MULTIPLICATION WORKBOOK

GRADE 3-5

THIS BOOK BELONGS TO:

TABLE OF CONTENTS

1)
$$\begin{array}{r} 0 \\ \times\ 7 \\ \hline \end{array}$$

2)
$$\begin{array}{r} 7 \\ \times\ 1 \\ \hline \end{array}$$

3)
$$\begin{array}{r} 1 \\ \times\ 5 \\ \hline \end{array}$$

4)
$$\begin{array}{r} 4 \\ \times\ 1 \\ \hline \end{array}$$

5)
$$\begin{array}{r} 0 \\ \times\ 9 \\ \hline \end{array}$$

6)
$$\begin{array}{r} 6 \\ \times\ 0 \\ \hline \end{array}$$

7)
$$\begin{array}{r} 0 \\ \times\ 2 \\ \hline \end{array}$$

8)
$$\begin{array}{r} 2 \\ \times\ 1 \\ \hline \end{array}$$

9)
$$\begin{array}{r} 0 \\ \times\ 4 \\ \hline \end{array}$$

10)
$$\begin{array}{r} 7 \\ \times\ 1 \\ \hline \end{array}$$

11)
$$\begin{array}{r} 0 \\ \times\ 7 \\ \hline \end{array}$$

12)
$$\begin{array}{r} 3 \\ \times\ 1 \\ \hline \end{array}$$

13)
$$\begin{array}{r} 1 \\ \times\ 3 \\ \hline \end{array}$$

14)
$$\begin{array}{r} 6 \\ \times\ 0 \\ \hline \end{array}$$

15)
$$\begin{array}{r} 0 \\ \times\ 1 \\ \hline \end{array}$$

16)
$$\begin{array}{r} 3 \\ \times\ 1 \\ \hline \end{array}$$

17)
$$\begin{array}{r} 0 \\ \times\ 7 \\ \hline \end{array}$$

18)
$$\begin{array}{r} 1 \\ \times\ 1 \\ \hline \end{array}$$

19)
$$\begin{array}{r} 1 \\ \times\ 8 \\ \hline \end{array}$$

20)
$$\begin{array}{r} 9 \\ \times\ 0 \\ \hline \end{array}$$

21)
$$\begin{array}{r} 1 \\ \times\ 5 \\ \hline \end{array}$$

22)
$$\begin{array}{r} 5 \\ \times\ 1 \\ \hline \end{array}$$

23)
$$\begin{array}{r} 0 \\ \times\ 8 \\ \hline \end{array}$$

24)
$$\begin{array}{r} 8 \\ \times\ 1 \\ \hline \end{array}$$

25)
$$\begin{array}{r} 0 \\ \times\ 2 \\ \hline \end{array}$$

26)
$$\begin{array}{r} 1 \\ \times\ 0 \\ \hline \end{array}$$

27)
$$\begin{array}{r} 0 \\ \times\ 1 \\ \hline \end{array}$$

28)
$$\begin{array}{r} 7 \\ \times\ 0 \\ \hline \end{array}$$

29)
$$\begin{array}{r} 0 \\ \times\ 2 \\ \hline \end{array}$$

30)
$$\begin{array}{r} 6 \\ \times\ 0 \\ \hline \end{array}$$

31)
$$\begin{array}{r} 0 \\ \times\ 3 \\ \hline \end{array}$$

32)
$$\begin{array}{r} 2 \\ \times\ 1 \\ \hline \end{array}$$

33)
$$\begin{array}{r} 0 \\ \times\ 6 \\ \hline \end{array}$$

34)
$$\begin{array}{r} 3 \\ \times\ 1 \\ \hline \end{array}$$

35)
$$\begin{array}{r} 1 \\ \times\ 7 \\ \hline \end{array}$$

36)
$$\begin{array}{r} 1 \\ \times\ 0 \\ \hline \end{array}$$

37)
$$\begin{array}{r} 0 \\ \times\ 1 \\ \hline \end{array}$$

38)
$$\begin{array}{r} 4 \\ \times\ 1 \\ \hline \end{array}$$

39)
$$\begin{array}{r} 1 \\ \times\ 3 \\ \hline \end{array}$$

40)
$$\begin{array}{r} 2 \\ \times\ 1 \\ \hline \end{array}$$

41)
$$\begin{array}{r} 0 \\ \times\ 8 \\ \hline \end{array}$$

42)
$$\begin{array}{r} 6 \\ \times\ 1 \\ \hline \end{array}$$

43)
$$\begin{array}{r} 1 \\ \times\ 4 \\ \hline \end{array}$$

44)
$$\begin{array}{r} 2 \\ \times\ 1 \\ \hline \end{array}$$

45)
$$\begin{array}{r} 0 \\ \times\ 3 \\ \hline \end{array}$$

46)
$$\begin{array}{r} 2 \\ \times\ 0 \\ \hline \end{array}$$

47)
$$\begin{array}{r} 1 \\ \times\ 1 \\ \hline \end{array}$$

48)
$$\begin{array}{r} 5 \\ \times\ 0 \\ \hline \end{array}$$

49)
$$\begin{array}{r} 0 \\ \times\ 0 \\ \hline \end{array}$$

50)
$$\begin{array}{r} 2 \\ \times\ 1 \\ \hline \end{array}$$

51)
$$\begin{array}{r} 0 \\ \times\ 0 \\ \hline \end{array}$$

52)
$$\begin{array}{r} 6 \\ \times\ 0 \\ \hline \end{array}$$

53)
$$\begin{array}{r} 1 \\ \times\ 7 \\ \hline \end{array}$$

54)
$$\begin{array}{r} 8 \\ \times\ 0 \\ \hline \end{array}$$

55)
$$\begin{array}{r} 0 \\ \times\ 2 \\ \hline \end{array}$$

56)
$$\begin{array}{r} 8 \\ \times\ 1 \\ \hline \end{array}$$

57)
$$\begin{array}{r} 0 \\ \times\ 1 \\ \hline \end{array}$$

58)
$$\begin{array}{r} 3 \\ \times\ 0 \\ \hline \end{array}$$

59)
$$\begin{array}{r} 1 \\ \times\ 0 \\ \hline \end{array}$$

60)
$$\begin{array}{r} 7 \\ \times\ 0 \\ \hline \end{array}$$

Name: _____

Let's Multiply 0 & 1

Day /100

Date: _____
Time: _____

Score /60

1) $\begin{array}{r} 1 \\ \times\ 3 \\ \hline \end{array}$	2) $\begin{array}{r} 8 \\ \times\ 0 \\ \hline \end{array}$	3) $\begin{array}{r} 0 \\ \times\ 6 \\ \hline \end{array}$	4) $\begin{array}{r} 3 \\ \times\ 0 \\ \hline \end{array}$	5) $\begin{array}{r} 1 \\ \times\ 0 \\ \hline \end{array}$	6) $\begin{array}{r} 8 \\ \times\ 0 \\ \hline \end{array}$
7) $\begin{array}{r} 1 \\ \times\ 5 \\ \hline \end{array}$	8) $\begin{array}{r} 1 \\ \times\ 0 \\ \hline \end{array}$	9) $\begin{array}{r} 1 \\ \times\ 3 \\ \hline \end{array}$	10) $\begin{array}{r} 9 \\ \times\ 1 \\ \hline \end{array}$	11) $\begin{array}{r} 0 \\ \times\ 6 \\ \hline \end{array}$	12) $\begin{array}{r} 6 \\ \times\ 1 \\ \hline \end{array}$
13) $\begin{array}{r} 1 \\ \times\ 2 \\ \hline \end{array}$	14) $\begin{array}{r} 4 \\ \times\ 1 \\ \hline \end{array}$	15) $\begin{array}{r} 1 \\ \times\ 6 \\ \hline \end{array}$	16) $\begin{array}{r} 5 \\ \times\ 1 \\ \hline \end{array}$	17) $\begin{array}{r} 0 \\ \times\ 0 \\ \hline \end{array}$	18) $\begin{array}{r} 8 \\ \times\ 1 \\ \hline \end{array}$
19) $\begin{array}{r} 0 \\ \times\ 8 \\ \hline \end{array}$	20) $\begin{array}{r} 6 \\ \times\ 0 \\ \hline \end{array}$	21) $\begin{array}{r} 0 \\ \times\ 8 \\ \hline \end{array}$	22) $\begin{array}{r} 9 \\ \times\ 1 \\ \hline \end{array}$	23) $\begin{array}{r} 0 \\ \times\ 0 \\ \hline \end{array}$	24) $\begin{array}{r} 5 \\ \times\ 1 \\ \hline \end{array}$
25) $\begin{array}{r} 0 \\ \times\ 5 \\ \hline \end{array}$	26) $\begin{array}{r} 2 \\ \times\ 0 \\ \hline \end{array}$	27) $\begin{array}{r} 1 \\ \times\ 8 \\ \hline \end{array}$	28) $\begin{array}{r} 6 \\ \times\ 1 \\ \hline \end{array}$	29) $\begin{array}{r} 1 \\ \times\ 9 \\ \hline \end{array}$	30) $\begin{array}{r} 5 \\ \times\ 0 \\ \hline \end{array}$
31) $\begin{array}{r} 0 \\ \times\ 8 \\ \hline \end{array}$	32) $\begin{array}{r} 4 \\ \times\ 1 \\ \hline \end{array}$	33) $\begin{array}{r} 1 \\ \times\ 6 \\ \hline \end{array}$	34) $\begin{array}{r} 5 \\ \times\ 1 \\ \hline \end{array}$	35) $\begin{array}{r} 0 \\ \times\ 9 \\ \hline \end{array}$	36) $\begin{array}{r} 7 \\ \times\ 1 \\ \hline \end{array}$
37) $\begin{array}{r} 1 \\ \times\ 0 \\ \hline \end{array}$	38) $\begin{array}{r} 9 \\ \times\ 0 \\ \hline \end{array}$	39) $\begin{array}{r} 0 \\ \times\ 9 \\ \hline \end{array}$	40) $\begin{array}{r} 1 \\ \times\ 1 \\ \hline \end{array}$	41) $\begin{array}{r} 0 \\ \times\ 7 \\ \hline \end{array}$	42) $\begin{array}{r} 4 \\ \times\ 0 \\ \hline \end{array}$
43) $\begin{array}{r} 1 \\ \times\ 4 \\ \hline \end{array}$	44) $\begin{array}{r} 4 \\ \times\ 0 \\ \hline \end{array}$	45) $\begin{array}{r} 0 \\ \times\ 7 \\ \hline \end{array}$	46) $\begin{array}{r} 3 \\ \times\ 1 \\ \hline \end{array}$	47) $\begin{array}{r} 1 \\ \times\ 8 \\ \hline \end{array}$	48) $\begin{array}{r} 9 \\ \times\ 1 \\ \hline \end{array}$
49) $\begin{array}{r} 1 \\ \times\ 4 \\ \hline \end{array}$	50) $\begin{array}{r} 3 \\ \times\ 1 \\ \hline \end{array}$	51) $\begin{array}{r} 1 \\ \times\ 8 \\ \hline \end{array}$	52) $\begin{array}{r} 0 \\ \times\ 0 \\ \hline \end{array}$	53) $\begin{array}{r} 1 \\ \times\ 0 \\ \hline \end{array}$	54) $\begin{array}{r} 2 \\ \times\ 0 \\ \hline \end{array}$
55) $\begin{array}{r} 1 \\ \times\ 7 \\ \hline \end{array}$	56) $\begin{array}{r} 2 \\ \times\ 1 \\ \hline \end{array}$	57) $\begin{array}{r} 1 \\ \times\ 3 \\ \hline \end{array}$	58) $\begin{array}{r} 2 \\ \times\ 1 \\ \hline \end{array}$	59) $\begin{array}{r} 1 \\ \times\ 3 \\ \hline \end{array}$	60) $\begin{array}{r} 3 \\ \times\ 1 \\ \hline \end{array}$

Name: _____

Let's Multiply 0 & 1

Day /100

Date: _____

Time: _____

Score /60

1)   1
  × 2

2)   1
  × 1

3)   1
  × 9

4)   0
  × 0

5)   0
  × 0

6)   7
  × 0

7)   1
  × 1

8)   4
  × 0

9)   0
  × 6

10)   0
  × 1

11)   0
  × 8

12)   0
  × 0

13)   1
  × 4

14)   7
  × 0

15)   0
  × 3

16)   7
  × 0

17)   1
  × 0

18)   9
  × 1

19)   1
  × 7

20)   4
  × 0

21)   1
  × 6

22)   8
  × 0

23)   1
  × 7

24)   0
  × 0

25)   1
  × 0

26)   4
  × 0

27)   0
  × 3

28)   3
  × 1

29)   1
  × 4

30)   8
  × 0

31)   0
  × 5

32)   8
  × 1

33)   1
  × 1

34)   0
  × 1

35)   0
  × 9

36)   3
  × 1

37)   0
  × 3

38)   3
  × 0

39)   1
  × 8

40)   0
  × 0

41)   1
  × 6

42)   3
  × 1

43)   0
  × 9

44)   7
  × 0

45)   0
  × 3

46)   6
  × 1

47)   0
  × 5

48)   6
  × 0

49)   0
  × 2

50)   7
  × 1

51)   0
  × 5

52)   1
  × 0

53)   0
  × 2

54)   8
  × 1

55)   0
  × 9

56)   5
  × 1

57)   0
  × 0

58)   6
  × 1

59)   0
  × 8

60)   4
  × 1

Name: _____

Let's Multiply 0 & 1

Day /100

Date: _____
Time: _____

Score /60

1)
$$\begin{array}{r} 0 \\ \times\ 2 \\ \hline \end{array}$$

2)
$$\begin{array}{r} 4 \\ \times\ 1 \\ \hline \end{array}$$

3)
$$\begin{array}{r} 1 \\ \times\ 8 \\ \hline \end{array}$$

4)
$$\begin{array}{r} 0 \\ \times\ 1 \\ \hline \end{array}$$

5)
$$\begin{array}{r} 1 \\ \times\ 1 \\ \hline \end{array}$$

6)
$$\begin{array}{r} 5 \\ \times\ 1 \\ \hline \end{array}$$

7)
$$\begin{array}{r} 0 \\ \times\ 2 \\ \hline \end{array}$$

8)
$$\begin{array}{r} 2 \\ \times\ 0 \\ \hline \end{array}$$

9)
$$\begin{array}{r} 1 \\ \times\ 6 \\ \hline \end{array}$$

10)
$$\begin{array}{r} 7 \\ \times\ 0 \\ \hline \end{array}$$

11)
$$\begin{array}{r} 0 \\ \times\ 1 \\ \hline \end{array}$$

12)
$$\begin{array}{r} 0 \\ \times\ 1 \\ \hline \end{array}$$

13)
$$\begin{array}{r} 1 \\ \times\ 0 \\ \hline \end{array}$$

14)
$$\begin{array}{r} 7 \\ \times\ 0 \\ \hline \end{array}$$

15)
$$\begin{array}{r} 1 \\ \times\ 8 \\ \hline \end{array}$$

16)
$$\begin{array}{r} 9 \\ \times\ 0 \\ \hline \end{array}$$

17)
$$\begin{array}{r} 0 \\ \times\ 0 \\ \hline \end{array}$$

18)
$$\begin{array}{r} 0 \\ \times\ 1 \\ \hline \end{array}$$

19)
$$\begin{array}{r} 0 \\ \times\ 2 \\ \hline \end{array}$$

20)
$$\begin{array}{r} 3 \\ \times\ 1 \\ \hline \end{array}$$

21)
$$\begin{array}{r} 1 \\ \times\ 3 \\ \hline \end{array}$$

22)
$$\begin{array}{r} 4 \\ \times\ 0 \\ \hline \end{array}$$

23)
$$\begin{array}{r} 0 \\ \times\ 3 \\ \hline \end{array}$$

24)
$$\begin{array}{r} 4 \\ \times\ 1 \\ \hline \end{array}$$

25)
$$\begin{array}{r} 1 \\ \times\ 6 \\ \hline \end{array}$$

26)
$$\begin{array}{r} 8 \\ \times\ 1 \\ \hline \end{array}$$

27)
$$\begin{array}{r} 0 \\ \times\ 7 \\ \hline \end{array}$$

28)
$$\begin{array}{r} 0 \\ \times\ 0 \\ \hline \end{array}$$

29)
$$\begin{array}{r} 1 \\ \times\ 7 \\ \hline \end{array}$$

30)
$$\begin{array}{r} 4 \\ \times\ 1 \\ \hline \end{array}$$

31)
$$\begin{array}{r} 0 \\ \times\ 5 \\ \hline \end{array}$$

32)
$$\begin{array}{r} 5 \\ \times\ 0 \\ \hline \end{array}$$

33)
$$\begin{array}{r} 0 \\ \times\ 3 \\ \hline \end{array}$$

34)
$$\begin{array}{r} 8 \\ \times\ 0 \\ \hline \end{array}$$

35)
$$\begin{array}{r} 1 \\ \times\ 6 \\ \hline \end{array}$$

36)
$$\begin{array}{r} 2 \\ \times\ 0 \\ \hline \end{array}$$

37)
$$\begin{array}{r} 0 \\ \times\ 5 \\ \hline \end{array}$$

38)
$$\begin{array}{r} 0 \\ \times\ 0 \\ \hline \end{array}$$

39)
$$\begin{array}{r} 0 \\ \times\ 2 \\ \hline \end{array}$$

40)
$$\begin{array}{r} 7 \\ \times\ 0 \\ \hline \end{array}$$

41)
$$\begin{array}{r} 0 \\ \times\ 0 \\ \hline \end{array}$$

42)
$$\begin{array}{r} 7 \\ \times\ 1 \\ \hline \end{array}$$

43)
$$\begin{array}{r} 1 \\ \times\ 2 \\ \hline \end{array}$$

44)
$$\begin{array}{r} 8 \\ \times\ 0 \\ \hline \end{array}$$

45)
$$\begin{array}{r} 1 \\ \times\ 4 \\ \hline \end{array}$$

46)
$$\begin{array}{r} 2 \\ \times\ 1 \\ \hline \end{array}$$

47)
$$\begin{array}{r} 0 \\ \times\ 8 \\ \hline \end{array}$$

48)
$$\begin{array}{r} 1 \\ \times\ 0 \\ \hline \end{array}$$

49)
$$\begin{array}{r} 0 \\ \times\ 8 \\ \hline \end{array}$$

50)
$$\begin{array}{r} 0 \\ \times\ 0 \\ \hline \end{array}$$

51)
$$\begin{array}{r} 0 \\ \times\ 5 \\ \hline \end{array}$$

52)
$$\begin{array}{r} 4 \\ \times\ 1 \\ \hline \end{array}$$

53)
$$\begin{array}{r} 1 \\ \times\ 9 \\ \hline \end{array}$$

54)
$$\begin{array}{r} 5 \\ \times\ 0 \\ \hline \end{array}$$

55)
$$\begin{array}{r} 0 \\ \times\ 9 \\ \hline \end{array}$$

56)
$$\begin{array}{r} 8 \\ \times\ 1 \\ \hline \end{array}$$

57)
$$\begin{array}{r} 1 \\ \times\ 5 \\ \hline \end{array}$$

58)
$$\begin{array}{r} 4 \\ \times\ 1 \\ \hline \end{array}$$

59)
$$\begin{array}{r} 1 \\ \times\ 4 \\ \hline \end{array}$$

60)
$$\begin{array}{r} 3 \\ \times\ 1 \\ \hline \end{array}$$

Name: _____

  Let's Multiply 0 & 1

Day /100

Date: _____
Time: _____

Score /60

1) 0
   × 7

2) 8
   × 0

3) 0
   × 9

4) 5
   × 1

5) 0
   × 6

6) 5
   × 1

7) 0
   × 2

8) 0
   × 0

9) 0
   × 6

10) 5
    × 1

11) 1
    × 8

12) 8
    × 1

13) 1
    × 6

14) 3
    × 0

15) 1
    × 6

16) 1
    × 1

17) 1
    × 4

18) 7
    × 1

19) 1
    × 8

20) 9
    × 1

21) 0
    × 1

22) 7
    × 1

23) 0
    × 4

24) 8
    × 0

25) 1
    × 2

26) 3
    × 1

27) 0
    × 8

28) 9
    × 1

29) 1
    × 8

30) 1
    × 1

31) 1
    × 2

32) 7
    × 1

33) 1
    × 7

34) 1
    × 1

35) 0
    × 9

36) 8
    × 0

37) 1
    × 5

38) 7
    × 1

39) 0
    × 9

40) 6
    × 1

41) 0
    × 5

42) 9
    × 1

43) 0
    × 2

44) 1
    × 0

45) 1
    × 6

46) 1
    × 1

47) 1
    × 9

48) 2
    × 1

49) 1
    × 3

50) 7
    × 0

51) 1
    × 6

52) 1
    × 1

53) 1
    × 2

54) 6
    × 0

55) 1
    × 0

56) 3
    × 0

57) 0
    × 5

58) 7
    × 0

59) 1
    × 5

60) 3
    × 1

Name: _____

Let's Multiply 2

Day /100

Date: _____

Time: _____

Score /60

1) 2
  × 3

2) 1
  × 2

3) 2
  × 9

4) 9
  × 2

5) 2
  × 0

6) 8
  × 2

7) 2
  × 0

8) 2
  × 2

9) 2
  × 3

10) 5
  × 2

11) 2
  × 6

12) 6
  × 2

13) 2
  × 7

14) 7
  × 2

15) 2
  × 7

16) 6
  × 2

17) 2
  × 8

18) 1
  × 2

19) 2
  × 2

20) 0
  × 2

21) 2
  × 3

22) 9
  × 2

23) 2
  × 2

24) 8
  × 2

25) 2
  × 1

26) 4
  × 2

27) 2
  × 0

28) 1
  × 2

29) 2
  × 4

30) 5
  × 2

31) 2
  × 8

32) 2
  × 2

33) 2
  × 2

34) 5
  × 2

35) 2
  × 3

36) 9
  × 2

37) 2
  × 9

38) 8
  × 2

39) 2
  × 1

40) 6
  × 2

41) 2
  × 1

42) 0
  × 2

43) 2
  × 9

44) 9
  × 2

45) 2
  × 5

46) 4
  × 2

47) 2
  × 2

48) 6
  × 2

49) 2
  × 4

50) 5
  × 2

51) 2
  × 8

52) 8
  × 2

53) 2
  × 1

54) 2
  × 2

55) 2
  × 5

56) 9
  × 2

57) 2
  × 2

58) 6
  × 2

59) 2
  × 2

60) 2
  × 2

1)   2 × 7

2)   3 × 2

3)   2 × 5

4)   0 × 2

5)   2 × 1

6)   8 × 2

7)   2 × 8

8)   1 × 2

9)   2 × 7

10)   6 × 2

11)   2 × 5

12)   3 × 2

13)   2 × 5

14)   1 × 2

15)   2 × 5

16)   6 × 2

17)   2 × 6

18)   2 × 2

19)   2 × 7

20)   5 × 2

21)   2 × 7

22)   3 × 2

23)   2 × 0

24)   6 × 2

25)   2 × 5

26)   5 × 2

27)   2 × 2

28)   8 × 2

29)   2 × 6

30)   2 × 2

31)   2 × 6

32)   9 × 2

33)   2 × 1

34)   3 × 2

35)   2 × 6

36)   5 × 2

37)   2 × 5

38)   9 × 2

39)   2 × 0

40)   0 × 2

41)   2 × 3

42)   2 × 2

43)   2 × 5

44)   2 × 2

45)   2 × 7

46)   4 × 2

47)   2 × 1

48)   9 × 2

49)   2 × 5

50)   1 × 2

51)   2 × 7

52)   4 × 2

53)   2 × 9

54)   8 × 2

55)   2 × 9

56)   0 × 2

57)   2 × 9

58)   3 × 2

59)   2 × 1

60)   4 × 2

Name: _____

Let's Multiply 2

Day /100

Date: _____
Time: _____

Score /60

1) 2 × 5

2) 4 × 2

3) 2 × 4

4) 0 × 2

5) 2 × 0

6) 5 × 2

7) 2 × 4

8) 3 × 2

9) 2 × 1

10) 4 × 2

11) 2 × 1

12) 3 × 2

13) 2 × 3

14) 9 × 2

15) 2 × 5

16) 4 × 2

17) 2 × 4

18) 2 × 2

19) 2 × 3

20) 5 × 2

21) 2 × 1

22) 7 × 2

23) 2 × 4

24) 9 × 2

25) 2 × 1

26) 2 × 2

27) 2 × 4

28) 3 × 2

29) 2 × 4

30) 6 × 2

31) 2 × 7

32) 6 × 2

33) 2 × 4

34) 6 × 2

35) 2 × 3

36) 8 × 2

37) 2 × 6

38) 5 × 2

39) 2 × 5

40) 5 × 2

41) 2 × 0

42) 3 × 2

43) 2 × 9

44) 5 × 2

45) 2 × 9

46) 1 × 2

47) 2 × 9

48) 5 × 2

49) 2 × 4

50) 6 × 2

51) 2 × 9

52) 2 × 2

53) 2 × 8

54) 4 × 2

55) 2 × 2

56) 6 × 2

57) 2 × 4

58) 0 × 2

59) 2 × 5

60) 9 × 2

1) 2 × 7

2) 7 × 2

3) 2 × 4

4) 0 × 2

5) 2 × 2

6) 6 × 2

7) 2 × 2

8) 2 × 2

9) 2 × 8

10) 6 × 2

11) 2 × 5

12) 2 × 2

13) 2 × 7

14) 3 × 2

15) 2 × 0

16) 6 × 2

17) 2 × 2

18) 6 × 2

19) 2 × 3

20) 1 × 2

21) 2 × 6

22) 2 × 2

23) 2 × 6

24) 6 × 2

25) 2 × 3

26) 5 × 2

27) 2 × 9

28) 6 × 2

29) 2 × 0

30) 0 × 2

31) 2 × 3

32) 7 × 2

33) 2 × 2

34) 0 × 2

35) 2 × 6

36) 9 × 2

37) 2 × 0

38) 2 × 2

39) 2 × 0

40) 9 × 2

41) 2 × 3

42) 1 × 2

43) 2 × 4

44) 7 × 2

45) 2 × 0

46) 6 × 2

47) 2 × 6

48) 4 × 2

49) 2 × 2

50) 3 × 2

51) 2 × 1

52) 9 × 2

53) 2 × 4

54) 5 × 2

55) 2 × 7

56) 8 × 2

57) 2 × 8

58) 2 × 2

59) 2 × 2

60) 0 × 2

Name: _____

Let's Multiply 2

Day /100

Date: _____
Time: _____

Score /60

1)   2
   × 2

2)   1
   × 2

3)   2
   × 1

4)   9
   × 2

5)   2
   × 5

6)   4
   × 2

7)   2
   × 7

8)   9
   × 2

9)   2
   × 9

10)   0
   × 2

11)   2
   × 3

12)   0
   × 2

13)   2
   × 4

14)   1
   × 2

15)   2
   × 2

16)   2
   × 2

17)   2
   × 0

18)   0
   × 2

19)   2
   × 9

20)   4
   × 2

21)   2
   × 9

22)   8
   × 2

23)   2
   × 7

24)   0
   × 2

25)   2
   × 2

26)   7
   × 2

27)   2
   × 0

28)   1
   × 2

29)   2
   × 1

30)   3
   × 2

31)   2
   × 2

32)   5
   × 2

33)   2
   × 0

34)   7
   × 2

35)   2
   × 3

36)   0
   × 2

37)   2
   × 3

38)   2
   × 2

39)   2
   × 7

40)   1
   × 2

41)   2
   × 6

42)   4
   × 2

43)   2
   × 5

44)   4
   × 2

45)   2
   × 4

46)   6
   × 2

47)   2
   × 3

48)   3
   × 2

49)   2
   × 7

50)   1
   × 2

51)   2
   × 5

52)   8
   × 2

53)   2
   × 0

54)   9
   × 2

55)   2
   × 0

56)   2
   × 2

57)   2
   × 0

58)   5
   × 2

59)   2
   × 4

60)   4
   × 2

Name: _____

Let's Multiply 2

Day /100

Date: _____
Time: _____

Score /60

1) 2
   × 3

2) 6
   × 2

3) 2
   × 2

4) 7
   × 2

5) 2
   × 7

6) 9
   × 2

7) 2
   × 3

8) 2
   × 2

9) 2
   × 6

10) 6
    × 2

11) 2
    × 3

12) 7
    × 2

13) 2
    × 0

14) 9
    × 2

15) 2
    × 7

16) 1
    × 2

17) 2
    × 0

18) 6
    × 2

19) 2
    × 4

20) 7
    × 2

21) 2
    × 7

22) 9
    × 2

23) 2
    × 7

24) 8
    × 2

25) 2
    × 3

26) 0
    × 2

27) 2
    × 5

28) 9
    × 2

29) 2
    × 5

30) 4
    × 2

31) 2
    × 1

32) 9
    × 2

33) 2
    × 1

34) 8
    × 2

35) 2
    × 7

36) 7
    × 2

37) 2
    × 4

38) 4
    × 2

39) 2
    × 3

40) 1
    × 2

41) 2
    × 7

42) 7
    × 2

43) 2
    × 2

44) 6
    × 2

45) 2
    × 4

46) 5
    × 2

47) 2
    × 8

48) 6
    × 2

49) 2
    × 2

50) 1
    × 2

51) 2
    × 5

52) 6
    × 2

53) 2
    × 9

54) 2
    × 2

55) 2
    × 5

56) 9
    × 2

57) 2
    × 1

58) 7
    × 2

59) 2
    × 4

60) 0
    × 2

Name: _____

Let's Multiply 2

Day /100

Date: _____
Time: _____

Score /60

1) 2 × 7

2) 1 × 2

3) 2 × 1

4) 1 × 2

5) 2 × 5

6) 7 × 2

7) 2 × 0

8) 5 × 2

9) 2 × 6

10) 4 × 2

11) 2 × 1

12) 6 × 2

13) 2 × 6

14) 2 × 2

15) 2 × 6

16) 8 × 2

17) 2 × 6

18) 9 × 2

19) 2 × 3

20) 9 × 2

21) 2 × 9

22) 4 × 2

23) 2 × 0

24) 3 × 2

25) 2 × 2

26) 7 × 2

27) 2 × 6

28) 9 × 2

29) 2 × 1

30) 3 × 2

31) 2 × 5

32) 6 × 2

33) 2 × 7

34) 2 × 2

35) 2 × 3

36) 5 × 2

37) 2 × 3

38) 4 × 2

39) 2 × 5

40) 4 × 2

41) 2 × 7

42) 8 × 2

43) 2 × 3

44) 5 × 2

45) 2 × 4

46) 2 × 2

47) 2 × 6

48) 3 × 2

49) 2 × 0

50) 1 × 2

51) 2 × 9

52) 1 × 2

53) 2 × 0

54) 0 × 2

55) 2 × 6

56) 2 × 2

57) 2 × 1

58) 2 × 2

59) 2 × 7

60) 0 × 2

1) 3 × 0

2) 9 × 3

3) 3 × 7

4) 2 × 3

5) 3 × 6

6) 8 × 3

7) 3 × 6

8) 7 × 3

9) 3 × 5

10) 4 × 3

11) 3 × 4

12) 7 × 3

13) 3 × 0

14) 9 × 3

15) 3 × 4

16) 3 × 3

17) 3 × 6

18) 1 × 3

19) 3 × 7

20) 3 × 3

21) 3 × 5

22) 8 × 3

23) 3 × 6

24) 4 × 3

25) 3 × 9

26) 7 × 3

27) 3 × 4

28) 9 × 3

29) 3 × 3

30) 6 × 3

31) 3 × 4

32) 5 × 3

33) 3 × 0

34) 3 × 3

35) 3 × 3

36) 8 × 3

37) 3 × 8

38) 4 × 3

39) 3 × 9

40) 9 × 3

41) 3 × 5

42) 6 × 3

43) 3 × 8

44) 8 × 3

45) 3 × 2

46) 5 × 3

47) 3 × 6

48) 3 × 3

49) 3 × 0

50) 6 × 3

51) 3 × 5

52) 2 × 3

53) 3 × 7

54) 8 × 3

55) 3 × 3

56) 6 × 3

57) 3 × 7

58) 7 × 3

59) 3 × 5

60) 2 × 3

Name: _____

Let's Multiply 3

Day /100

Date: _____
Time: _____

Score /60

1) 3
   × 3

2) 5
   × 3

3) 3
   × 2

4) 3
   × 3

5) 3
   × 0

6) 6
   × 3

7) 3
   × 7

8) 5
   × 3

9) 3
   × 3

10) 8
    × 3

11) 3
    × 8

12) 6
    × 3

13) 3
    × 0

14) 8
    × 3

15) 3
    × 2

16) 4
    × 3

17) 3
    × 7

18) 8
    × 3

19) 3
    × 3

20) 6
    × 3

21) 3
    × 7

22) 5
    × 3

23) 3
    × 6

24) 6
    × 3

25) 3
    × 7

26) 3
    × 3

27) 3
    × 7

28) 6
    × 3

29) 3
    × 5

30) 8
    × 3

31) 3
    × 4

32) 5
    × 3

33) 3
    × 0

34) 6
    × 3

35) 3
    × 4

36) 7
    × 3

37) 3
    × 9

38) 0
    × 3

39) 3
    × 9

40) 8
    × 3

41) 3
    × 3

42) 4
    × 3

43) 3
    × 2

44) 2
    × 3

45) 3
    × 1

46) 8
    × 3

47) 3
    × 3

48) 8
    × 3

49) 3
    × 7

50) 8
    × 3

51) 3
    × 7

52) 4
    × 3

53) 3
    × 3

54) 3
    × 3

55) 3
    × 5

56) 4
    × 3

57) 3
    × 5

58) 0
    × 3

59) 3
    × 6

60) 0
    × 3

Name: _____

Let's Multiply 3

Day /100

Date: _____
Time: _____

Score /60

1) 3
× 6

2) 7
× 3

3) 3
× 4

4) 7
× 3

5) 3
× 6

6) 2
× 3

7) 3
× 8

8) 0
× 3

9) 3
× 7

10) 0
× 3

11) 3
× 8

12) 6
× 3

13) 3
× 3

14) 4
× 3

15) 3
× 7

16) 0
× 3

17) 3
× 7

18) 7
× 3

19) 3
× 4

20) 4
× 3

21) 3
× 0

22) 6
× 3

23) 3
× 5

24) 4
× 3

25) 3
× 0

26) 8
× 3

27) 3
× 9

28) 2
× 3

29) 3
× 6

30) 3
× 3

31) 3
× 9

32) 6
× 3

33) 3
× 6

34) 3
× 3

35) 3
× 3

36) 6
× 3

37) 3
× 1

38) 5
× 3

39) 3
× 0

40) 7
× 3

41) 3
× 9

42) 3
× 3

43) 3
× 3

44) 3
× 3

45) 3
× 0

46) 4
× 3

47) 3
× 8

48) 5
× 3

49) 3
× 6

50) 2
× 3

51) 3
× 8

52) 7
× 3

53) 3
× 6

54) 1
× 3

55) 3
× 5

56) 1
× 3

57) 3
× 5

58) 5
× 3

59) 3
× 4

60) 9
× 3

Name: _____

Let's Multiply 3

Day /100

Date: _____
Time: _____

Score /60

1)   3
   × 0

2)   8
   × 3

3)   3
   × 7

4)   8
   × 3

5)   3
   × 6

6)   8
   × 3

7)   3
   × 9

8)   9
   × 3

9)   3
   × 4

10)   0
    × 3

11)   3
    × 9

12)   3
    × 3

13)   3
    × 6

14)   5
    × 3

15)   3
    × 7

16)   7
    × 3

17)   3
    × 4

18)   9
    × 3

19)   3
    × 0

20)   5
    × 3

21)   3
    × 9

22)   1
    × 3

23)   3
    × 1

24)   7
    × 3

25)   3
    × 9

26)   0
    × 3

27)   3
    × 3

28)   2
    × 3

29)   3
    × 1

30)   0
    × 3

31)   3
    × 2

32)   4
    × 3

33)   3
    × 5

34)   6
    × 3

35)   3
    × 7

36)   8
    × 3

37)   3
    × 6

38)   3
    × 3

39)   3
    × 9

40)   1
    × 3

41)   3
    × 4

42)   2
    × 3

43)   3
    × 1

44)   5
    × 3

45)   3
    × 7

46)   3
    × 3

47)   3
    × 8

48)   8
    × 3

49)   3
    × 5

50)   5
    × 3

51)   3
    × 2

52)   2
    × 3

53)   3
    × 8

54)   2
    × 3

55)   3
    × 4

56)   9
    × 3

57)   3
    × 3

58)   0
    × 3

59)   3
    × 2

60)   5
    × 3

Name: _____

Let's Multiply 3

Day /100

Date: _____
Time: _____

Score /60

1) 3 × 2

2) 4 × 3

3) 3 × 3

4) 0 × 3

5) 3 × 7

6) 2 × 3

7) 3 × 2

8) 1 × 3

9) 3 × 3

10) 0 × 3

11) 3 × 4

12) 0 × 3

13) 3 × 7

14) 8 × 3

15) 3 × 9

16) 5 × 3

17) 3 × 5

18) 9 × 3

19) 3 × 8

20) 1 × 3

21) 3 × 0

22) 2 × 3

23) 3 × 6

24) 5 × 3

25) 3 × 4

26) 5 × 3

27) 3 × 0

28) 7 × 3

29) 3 × 2

30) 4 × 3

31) 3 × 6

32) 0 × 3

33) 3 × 2

34) 9 × 3

35) 3 × 8

36) 6 × 3

37) 3 × 7

38) 6 × 3

39) 3 × 6

40) 6 × 3

41) 3 × 5

42) 9 × 3

43) 3 × 9

44) 9 × 3

45) 3 × 0

46) 6 × 3

47) 3 × 2

48) 2 × 3

49) 3 × 5

50) 6 × 3

51) 3 × 9

52) 7 × 3

53) 3 × 1

54) 2 × 3

55) 3 × 4

56) 2 × 3

57) 3 × 7

58) 8 × 3

59) 3 × 2

60) 8 × 3

Name: _____

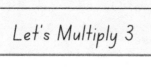 Let's Multiply 3

Day /100

Date: _____

Time: _____

Score /60

1)   3
   × 5

2)   5
   × 3

3)   3
   × 2

4)   1
   × 3

5)   3
   × 3

6)   4
   × 3

7)   3
   × 7

8)   8
   × 3

9)   3
   × 9

10)   8
   × 3

11)   3
   × 7

12)   3
   × 3

13)   3
   × 9

14)   2
   × 3

15)   3
   × 5

16)   7
   × 3

17)   3
   × 0

18)   6
   × 3

19)   3
   × 2

20)   7
   × 3

21)   3
   × 5

22)   2
   × 3

23)   3
   × 1

24)   4
   × 3

25)   3
   × 8

26)   6
   × 3

27)   3
   × 8

28)   5
   × 3

29)   3
   × 6

30)   5
   × 3

31)   3
   × 5

32)   0
   × 3

33)   3
   × 6

34)   5
   × 3

35)   3
   × 2

36)   4
   × 3

37)   3
   × 3

38)   1
   × 3

39)   3
   × 5

40)   4
   × 3

41)   3
   × 2

42)   0
   × 3

43)   3
   × 0

44)   2
   × 3

45)   3
   × 8

46)   3
   × 3

47)   3
   × 5

48)   3
   × 3

49)   3
   × 7

50)   4
   × 3

51)   3
   × 4

52)   4
   × 3

53)   3
   × 9

54)   4
   × 3

55)   3
   × 8

56)   3
   × 3

57)   3
   × 7

58)   1
   × 3

59)   3
   × 6

60)   6
   × 3

Name: _____

Let's Multiply 3

Day /100

Date: _____
Time: _____

Score /60

1)
```
  3
× 8
```

2)
```
  8
× 3
```

3)
```
  3
× 0
```

4)
```
  4
× 3
```

5)
```
  3
× 8
```

6)
```
  4
× 3
```

7)
```
  3
× 8
```

8)
```
  3
× 3
```

9)
```
  3
× 9
```

10)
```
  8
× 3
```

11)
```
  3
× 3
```

12)
```
  6
× 3
```

13)
```
  3
× 7
```

14)
```
  1
× 3
```

15)
```
  3
× 3
```

16)
```
  7
× 3
```

17)
```
  3
× 4
```

18)
```
  4
× 3
```

19)
```
  3
× 6
```

20)
```
  2
× 3
```

21)
```
  3
× 2
```

22)
```
  2
× 3
```

23)
```
  3
× 5
```

24)
```
  8
× 3
```

25)
```
  3
× 0
```

26)
```
  9
× 3
```

27)
```
  3
× 6
```

28)
```
  2
× 3
```

29)
```
  3
× 5
```

30)
```
  5
× 3
```

31)
```
  3
× 2
```

32)
```
  0
× 3
```

33)
```
  3
× 2
```

34)
```
  3
× 3
```

35)
```
  3
× 2
```

36)
```
  4
× 3
```

37)
```
  3
× 9
```

38)
```
  5
× 3
```

39)
```
  3
× 1
```

40)
```
  8
× 3
```

41)
```
  3
× 7
```

42)
```
  7
× 3
```

43)
```
  3
× 1
```

44)
```
  9
× 3
```

45)
```
  3
× 5
```

46)
```
  5
× 3
```

47)
```
  3
× 3
```

48)
```
  9
× 3
```

49)
```
  3
× 0
```

50)
```
  0
× 3
```

51)
```
  3
× 5
```

52)
```
  7
× 3
```

53)
```
  3
× 9
```

54)
```
  5
× 3
```

55)
```
  3
× 7
```

56)
```
  0
× 3
```

57)
```
  3
× 5
```

58)
```
  3
× 3
```

59)
```
  3
× 6
```

60)
```
  8
× 3
```

Name: _____

Let's Multiply 4

Day
/100

Date: _____
Time: _____

Score
/60

1) 4
  × 1

2) 2
  × 4

3) 4
  × 6

4) 4
  × 4

5) 4
  × 1

6) 2
  × 4

7) 4
  × 5

8) 6
  × 4

9) 4
  × 5

10) 6
  × 4

11) 4
  × 6

12) 5
  × 4

13) 4
  × 8

14) 8
  × 4

15) 4
  × 7

16) 9
  × 4

17) 4
  × 8

18) 0
  × 4

19) 4
  × 2

20) 2
  × 4

21) 4
  × 9

22) 0
  × 4

23) 4
  × 6

24) 9
  × 4

25) 4
  × 2

26) 4
  × 4

27) 4
  × 4

28) 1
  × 4

29) 4
  × 7

30) 6
  × 4

31) 4
  × 9

32) 5
  × 4

33) 4
  × 3

34) 3
  × 4

35) 4
  × 9

36) 3
  × 4

37) 4
  × 0

38) 6
  × 4

39) 4
  × 9

40) 5
  × 4

41) 4
  × 1

42) 1
  × 4

43) 4
  × 4

44) 0
  × 4

45) 4
  × 5

46) 6
  × 4

47) 4
  × 3

48) 1
  × 4

49) 4
  × 8

50) 3
  × 4

51) 4
  × 1

52) 6
  × 4

53) 4
  × 8

54) 9
  × 4

55) 4
  × 8

56) 9
  × 4

57) 4
  × 1

58) 6
  × 4

59) 4
  × 6

60) 1
  × 4

Name: _____

Let's Multiply 4

Day /100

Date: _____
Time: _____

Score /60

1) 4 × 8

2) 2 × 4

3) 4 × 6

4) 9 × 4

5) 4 × 9

6) 3 × 4

7) 4 × 8

8) 7 × 4

9) 4 × 7

10) 4 × 4

11) 4 × 3

12) 4 × 4

13) 4 × 9

14) 2 × 4

15) 4 × 1

16) 1 × 4

17) 4 × 1

18) 6 × 4

19) 4 × 2

20) 4 × 4

21) 4 × 8

22) 3 × 4

23) 4 × 8

24) 1 × 4

25) 4 × 1

26) 2 × 4

27) 4 × 8

28) 4 × 4

29) 4 × 0

30) 1 × 4

31) 4 × 7

32) 5 × 4

33) 4 × 6

34) 0 × 4

35) 4 × 0

36) 6 × 4

37) 4 × 4

38) 3 × 4

39) 4 × 9

40) 8 × 4

41) 4 × 8

42) 7 × 4

43) 4 × 5

44) 9 × 4

45) 4 × 7

46) 1 × 4

47) 4 × 1

48) 1 × 4

49) 4 × 7

50) 5 × 4

51) 4 × 0

52) 8 × 4

53) 4 × 9

54) 4 × 4

55) 4 × 2

56) 0 × 4

57) 4 × 3

58) 0 × 4

59) 4 × 5

60) 9 × 4

Name: _____

Let's Multiply 4

Day /100

Date: _____
Time: _____

Score /60

1)   4
   × 7

2)   3
   × 4

3)   4
   × 2

4)   8
   × 4

5)   4
   × 7

6)   7
   × 4

7)   4
   × 0

8)   3
   × 4

9)   4
   × 1

10)   4
    × 4

11)   4
    × 8

12)   8
    × 4

13)   4
    × 4

14)   2
    × 4

15)   4
    × 8

16)   8
    × 4

17)   4
    × 5

18)   4
    × 4

19)   4
    × 1

20)   6
    × 4

21)   4
    × 5

22)   8
    × 4

23)   4
    × 4

24)   0
    × 4

25)   4
    × 6

26)   5
    × 4

27)   4
    × 1

28)   8
    × 4

29)   4
    × 4

30)   2
    × 4

31)   4
    × 1

32)   1
    × 4

33)   4
    × 5

34)   4
    × 4

35)   4
    × 8

36)   5
    × 4

37)   4
    × 1

38)   0
    × 4

39)   4
    × 7

40)   6
    × 4

41)   4
    × 3

42)   4
    × 4

43)   4
    × 3

44)   0
    × 4

45)   4
    × 4

46)   5
    × 4

47)   4
    × 3

48)   0
    × 4

49)   4
    × 4

50)   7
    × 4

51)   4
    × 7

52)   7
    × 4

53)   4
    × 5

54)   8
    × 4

55)   4
    × 4

56)   4
    × 4

57)   4
    × 8

58)   5
    × 4

59)   4
    × 7

60)   2
    × 4

1) 4 × 5

2) 2 × 4

3) 4 × 9

4) 2 × 4

5) 4 × 1

6) 7 × 4

7) 4 × 4

8) 3 × 4

9) 4 × 4

10) 6 × 4

11) 4 × 8

12) 9 × 4

13) 4 × 2

14) 4 × 4

15) 4 × 8

16) 6 × 4

17) 4 × 6

18) 5 × 4

19) 4 × 9

20) 7 × 4

21) 4 × 3

22) 8 × 4

23) 4 × 6

24) 1 × 4

25) 4 × 5

26) 0 × 4

27) 4 × 0

28) 0 × 4

29) 4 × 8

30) 7 × 4

31) 4 × 4

32) 8 × 4

33) 4 × 6

34) 0 × 4

35) 4 × 3

36) 2 × 4

37) 4 × 4

38) 1 × 4

39) 4 × 2

40) 9 × 4

41) 4 × 5

42) 6 × 4

43) 4 × 5

44) 9 × 4

45) 4 × 8

46) 7 × 4

47) 4 × 3

48) 9 × 4

49) 4 × 3

50) 1 × 4

51) 4 × 6

52) 4 × 4

53) 4 × 1

54) 8 × 4

55) 4 × 5

56) 5 × 4

57) 4 × 0

58) 4 × 4

59) 4 × 3

60) 1 × 4

Name: _____

Let's Multiply 4

Day /100

Date: _____
Time: _____

Score /60

1) 4
  × 1

2) 0
  × 4

3) 4
  × 5

4) 8
  × 4

5) 4
  × 9

6) 6
  × 4

7) 4
  × 2

8) 1
  × 4

9) 4
  × 2

10) 4
  × 4

11) 4
  × 7

12) 8
  × 4

13) 4
  × 3

14) 6
  × 4

15) 4
  × 2

16) 1
  × 4

17) 4
  × 5

18) 9
  × 4

19) 4
  × 3

20) 7
  × 4

21) 4
  × 0

22) 0
  × 4

23) 4
  × 6

24) 4
  × 4

25) 4
  × 0

26) 9
  × 4

27) 4
  × 7

28) 2
  × 4

29) 4
  × 4

30) 7
  × 4

31) 4
  × 8

32) 4
  × 4

33) 4
  × 9

34) 0
  × 4

35) 4
  × 9

36) 3
  × 4

37) 4
  × 5

38) 6
  × 4

39) 4
  × 2

40) 7
  × 4

41) 4
  × 4

42) 8
  × 4

43) 4
  × 7

44) 1
  × 4

45) 4
  × 7

46) 3
  × 4

47) 4
  × 3

48) 4
  × 4

49) 4
  × 1

50) 6
  × 4

51) 4
  × 6

52) 4
  × 4

53) 4
  × 0

54) 6
  × 4

55) 4
  × 0

56) 9
  × 4

57) 4
  × 9

58) 3
  × 4

59) 4
  × 8

60) 4
  × 4

1)
   4
× 3

2)
   0
× 4

3)
   4
× 3

4)
   9
× 4

5)
   4
× 6

6)
   6
× 4

7)
   4
× 3

8)
   5
× 4

9)
   4
× 9

10)
   7
× 4

11)
   4
× 5

12)
   3
× 4

13)
   4
× 2

14)
   2
× 4

15)
   4
× 0

16)
   4
× 4

17)
   4
× 5

18)
   8
× 4

19)
   4
× 0

20)
   0
× 4

21)
   4
× 0

22)
   5
× 4

23)
   4
× 4

24)
   5
× 4

25)
   4
× 9

26)
   5
× 4

27)
   4
× 2

28)
   2
× 4

29)
   4
× 2

30)
   5
× 4

31)
   4
× 4

32)
   5
× 4

33)
   4
× 1

34)
   2
× 4

35)
   4
× 0

36)
   9
× 4

37)
   4
× 2

38)
   0
× 4

39)
   4
× 6

40)
   2
× 4

41)
   4
× 5

42)
   2
× 4

43)
   4
× 3

44)
   6
× 4

45)
   4
× 0

46)
   9
× 4

47)
   4
× 4

48)
   5
× 4

49)
   4
× 3

50)
   4
× 4

51)
   4
× 2

52)
   7
× 4

53)
   4
× 3

54)
   4
× 4

55)
   4
× 5

56)
   0
× 4

57)
   4
× 6

58)
   1
× 4

59)
   4
× 4

60)
   3
× 4

1) 4 × 5

2) 2 × 4

3) 4 × 9

4) 2 × 4

5) 4 × 1

6) 4 × 4

7) 4 × 2

8) 8 × 4

9) 4 × 9

10) 8 × 4

11) 4 × 1

12) 2 × 4

13) 4 × 3

14) 9 × 4

15) 4 × 7

16) 8 × 4

17) 4 × 2

18) 2 × 4

19) 4 × 5

20) 7 × 4

21) 4 × 0

22) 9 × 4

23) 4 × 7

24) 6 × 4

25) 4 × 4

26) 7 × 4

27) 4 × 8

28) 7 × 4

29) 4 × 9

30) 6 × 4

31) 4 × 4

32) 6 × 4

33) 4 × 8

34) 7 × 4

35) 4 × 7

36) 5 × 4

37) 4 × 0

38) 4 × 4

39) 4 × 1

40) 6 × 4

41) 4 × 9

42) 0 × 4

43) 4 × 8

44) 9 × 4

45) 4 × 0

46) 3 × 4

47) 4 × 8

48) 1 × 4

49) 4 × 7

50) 4 × 4

51) 4 × 6

52) 1 × 4

53) 4 × 7

54) 9 × 4

55) 4 × 2

56) 1 × 4

57) 4 × 1

58) 9 × 4

59) 4 × 6

60) 6 × 4

Name: _____

Let's Multiply 5

Day
/100

Date: _____
Time: _____

Score
/60

1)   5
  × 1

2)   0
  × 5

3)   5
  × 4

4)   7
  × 5

5)   5
  × 4

6)   9
  × 5

7)   5
  × 7

8)   0
  × 5

9)   5
  × 3

10)   9
  × 5

11)   5
  × 7

12)   3
  × 5

13)   5
  × 4

14)   7
  × 5

15)   5
  × 8

16)   3
  × 5

17)   5
  × 5

18)   9
  × 5

19)   5
  × 9

20)   7
  × 5

21)   5
  × 2

22)   4
  × 5

23)   5
  × 1

24)   4
  × 5

25)   5
  × 2

26)   6
  × 5

27)   5
  × 0

28)   1
  × 5

29)   5
  × 4

30)   6
  × 5

31)   5
  × 0

32)   0
  × 5

33)   5
  × 1

34)   8
  × 5

35)   5
  × 0

36)   4
  × 5

37)   5
  × 8

38)   9
  × 5

39)   5
  × 0

40)   0
  × 5

41)   5
  × 9

42)   0
  × 5

43)   5
  × 4

44)   6
  × 5

45)   5
  × 5

46)   2
  × 5

47)   5
  × 2

48)   8
  × 5

49)   5
  × 9

50)   2
  × 5

51)   5
  × 0

52)   5
  × 5

53)   5
  × 8

54)   1
  × 5

55)   5
  × 9

56)   7
  × 5

57)   5
  × 5

58)   5
  × 5

59)   5
  × 3

60)   4
  × 5

1) $\begin{array}{r} 5 \\ \times\ 9 \\ \hline \end{array}$
2) $\begin{array}{r} 8 \\ \times\ 5 \\ \hline \end{array}$
3) $\begin{array}{r} 5 \\ \times\ 8 \\ \hline \end{array}$
4) $\begin{array}{r} 1 \\ \times\ 5 \\ \hline \end{array}$
5) $\begin{array}{r} 5 \\ \times\ 1 \\ \hline \end{array}$
6) $\begin{array}{r} 3 \\ \times\ 5 \\ \hline \end{array}$

7) $\begin{array}{r} 5 \\ \times\ 6 \\ \hline \end{array}$
8) $\begin{array}{r} 4 \\ \times\ 5 \\ \hline \end{array}$
9) $\begin{array}{r} 5 \\ \times\ 0 \\ \hline \end{array}$
10) $\begin{array}{r} 8 \\ \times\ 5 \\ \hline \end{array}$
11) $\begin{array}{r} 5 \\ \times\ 6 \\ \hline \end{array}$
12) $\begin{array}{r} 3 \\ \times\ 5 \\ \hline \end{array}$

13) $\begin{array}{r} 5 \\ \times\ 7 \\ \hline \end{array}$
14) $\begin{array}{r} 4 \\ \times\ 5 \\ \hline \end{array}$
15) $\begin{array}{r} 5 \\ \times\ 6 \\ \hline \end{array}$
16) $\begin{array}{r} 7 \\ \times\ 5 \\ \hline \end{array}$
17) $\begin{array}{r} 5 \\ \times\ 5 \\ \hline \end{array}$
18) $\begin{array}{r} 5 \\ \times\ 5 \\ \hline \end{array}$

19) $\begin{array}{r} 5 \\ \times\ 2 \\ \hline \end{array}$
20) $\begin{array}{r} 9 \\ \times\ 5 \\ \hline \end{array}$
21) $\begin{array}{r} 5 \\ \times\ 6 \\ \hline \end{array}$
22) $\begin{array}{r} 4 \\ \times\ 5 \\ \hline \end{array}$
23) $\begin{array}{r} 5 \\ \times\ 5 \\ \hline \end{array}$
24) $\begin{array}{r} 7 \\ \times\ 5 \\ \hline \end{array}$

25) $\begin{array}{r} 5 \\ \times\ 0 \\ \hline \end{array}$
26) $\begin{array}{r} 0 \\ \times\ 5 \\ \hline \end{array}$
27) $\begin{array}{r} 5 \\ \times\ 3 \\ \hline \end{array}$
28) $\begin{array}{r} 2 \\ \times\ 5 \\ \hline \end{array}$
29) $\begin{array}{r} 5 \\ \times\ 8 \\ \hline \end{array}$
30) $\begin{array}{r} 6 \\ \times\ 5 \\ \hline \end{array}$

31) $\begin{array}{r} 5 \\ \times\ 6 \\ \hline \end{array}$
32) $\begin{array}{r} 5 \\ \times\ 5 \\ \hline \end{array}$
33) $\begin{array}{r} 5 \\ \times\ 1 \\ \hline \end{array}$
34) $\begin{array}{r} 3 \\ \times\ 5 \\ \hline \end{array}$
35) $\begin{array}{r} 5 \\ \times\ 8 \\ \hline \end{array}$
36) $\begin{array}{r} 5 \\ \times\ 5 \\ \hline \end{array}$

37) $\begin{array}{r} 5 \\ \times\ 8 \\ \hline \end{array}$
38) $\begin{array}{r} 8 \\ \times\ 5 \\ \hline \end{array}$
39) $\begin{array}{r} 5 \\ \times\ 9 \\ \hline \end{array}$
40) $\begin{array}{r} 1 \\ \times\ 5 \\ \hline \end{array}$
41) $\begin{array}{r} 5 \\ \times\ 7 \\ \hline \end{array}$
42) $\begin{array}{r} 5 \\ \times\ 5 \\ \hline \end{array}$

43) $\begin{array}{r} 5 \\ \times\ 6 \\ \hline \end{array}$
44) $\begin{array}{r} 5 \\ \times\ 5 \\ \hline \end{array}$
45) $\begin{array}{r} 5 \\ \times\ 7 \\ \hline \end{array}$
46) $\begin{array}{r} 9 \\ \times\ 5 \\ \hline \end{array}$
47) $\begin{array}{r} 5 \\ \times\ 0 \\ \hline \end{array}$
48) $\begin{array}{r} 8 \\ \times\ 5 \\ \hline \end{array}$

49) $\begin{array}{r} 5 \\ \times\ 1 \\ \hline \end{array}$
50) $\begin{array}{r} 6 \\ \times\ 5 \\ \hline \end{array}$
51) $\begin{array}{r} 5 \\ \times\ 8 \\ \hline \end{array}$
52) $\begin{array}{r} 8 \\ \times\ 5 \\ \hline \end{array}$
53) $\begin{array}{r} 5 \\ \times\ 1 \\ \hline \end{array}$
54) $\begin{array}{r} 7 \\ \times\ 5 \\ \hline \end{array}$

55) $\begin{array}{r} 5 \\ \times\ 1 \\ \hline \end{array}$
56) $\begin{array}{r} 9 \\ \times\ 5 \\ \hline \end{array}$
57) $\begin{array}{r} 5 \\ \times\ 6 \\ \hline \end{array}$
58) $\begin{array}{r} 9 \\ \times\ 5 \\ \hline \end{array}$
59) $\begin{array}{r} 5 \\ \times\ 5 \\ \hline \end{array}$
60) $\begin{array}{r} 4 \\ \times\ 5 \\ \hline \end{array}$

1) 5 × 4

2) 6 × 5

3) 5 × 6

4) 2 × 5

5) 5 × 3

6) 6 × 5

7) 5 × 4

8) 3 × 5

9) 5 × 5

10) 1 × 5

11) 5 × 4

12) 7 × 5

13) 5 × 8

14) 0 × 5

15) 5 × 8

16) 6 × 5

17) 5 × 7

18) 8 × 5

19) 5 × 4

20) 0 × 5

21) 5 × 0

22) 9 × 5

23) 5 × 1

24) 7 × 5

25) 5 × 7

26) 6 × 5

27) 5 × 6

28) 6 × 5

29) 5 × 8

30) 9 × 5

31) 5 × 5

32) 1 × 5

33) 5 × 4

34) 8 × 5

35) 5 × 4

36) 7 × 5

37) 5 × 5

38) 2 × 5

39) 5 × 8

40) 0 × 5

41) 5 × 3

42) 3 × 5

43) 5 × 8

44) 0 × 5

45) 5 × 9

46) 6 × 5

47) 5 × 0

48) 3 × 5

49) 5 × 0

50) 3 × 5

51) 5 × 5

52) 1 × 5

53) 5 × 2

54) 5 × 5

55) 5 × 6

56) 7 × 5

57) 5 × 4

58) 0 × 5

59) 5 × 1

60) 1 × 5

Name: _____

 Let's Multiply 5

Day
/100

Date: _____
Time: _____

Score
/60

1)   5
  × 1

2)   2
  × 5

3)   5
  × 2

4)   3
  × 5

5)   5
  × 5

6)   7
  × 5

7)   5
  × 7

8)   5
  × 5

9)   5
  × 6

10)   3
  × 5

11)   5
  × 4

12)   3
  × 5

13)   5
  × 3

14)   1
  × 5

15)   5
  × 6

16)   1
  × 5

17)   5
  × 9

18)   4
  × 5

19)   5
  × 5

20)   4
  × 5

21)   5
  × 1

22)   6
  × 5

23)   5
  × 9

24)   0
  × 5

25)   5
  × 5

26)   6
  × 5

27)   5
  × 0

28)   0
  × 5

29)   5
  × 1

30)   9
  × 5

31)   5
  × 5

32)   9
  × 5

33)   5
  × 1

34)   1
  × 5

35)   5
  × 0

36)   3
  × 5

37)   5
  × 0

38)   9
  × 5

39)   5
  × 3

40)   5
  × 5

41)   5
  × 9

42)   7
  × 5

43)   5
  × 1

44)   9
  × 5

45)   5
  × 4

46)   6
  × 5

47)   5
  × 6

48)   5
  × 5

49)   5
  × 6

50)   4
  × 5

51)   5
  × 6

52)   0
  × 5

53)   5
  × 9

54)   2
  × 5

55)   5
  × 0

56)   8
  × 5

57)   5
  × 0

58)   5
  × 5

59)   5
  × 7

60)   1
  × 5

1) 5
  × 4

2) 9
  × 5

3) 5
  × 2

4) 1
  × 5

5) 5
  × 9

6) 4
  × 5

7) 5
  × 9

8) 6
  × 5

9) 5
  × 0

10) 1
  × 5

11) 5
  × 4

12) 1
  × 5

13) 5
  × 7

14) 3
  × 5

15) 5
  × 3

16) 3
  × 5

17) 5
  × 1

18) 5
  × 5

19) 5
  × 5

20) 2
  × 5

21) 5
  × 4

22) 8
  × 5

23) 5
  × 8

24) 6
  × 5

25) 5
  × 2

26) 1
  × 5

27) 5
  × 8

28) 8
  × 5

29) 5
  × 4

30) 7
  × 5

31) 5
  × 4

32) 7
  × 5

33) 5
  × 0

34) 1
  × 5

35) 5
  × 4

36) 1
  × 5

37) 5
  × 6

38) 5
  × 5

39) 5
  × 8

40) 6
  × 5

41) 5
  × 9

42) 4
  × 5

43) 5
  × 3

44) 4
  × 5

45) 5
  × 4

46) 4
  × 5

47) 5
  × 9

48) 0
  × 5

49) 5
  × 9

50) 4
  × 5

51) 5
  × 3

52) 2
  × 5

53) 5
  × 9

54) 0
  × 5

55) 5
  × 2

56) 5
  × 5

57) 5
  × 0

58) 5
  × 5

59) 5
  × 2

60) 8
  × 5

Name: _____

Let's Multiply 5

Day
/100

Date: _____
Time: _____

Score
/60

1) 5
   × 7

2) 1
   × 5

3) 5
   × 3

4) 9
   × 5

5) 5
   × 5

6) 1
   × 5

7) 5
   × 1

8) 9
   × 5

9) 5
   × 0

10) 7
    × 5

11) 5
    × 9

12) 3
    × 5

13) 5
    × 6

14) 4
    × 5

15) 5
    × 2

16) 0
    × 5

17) 5
    × 2

18) 3
    × 5

19) 5
    × 5

20) 9
    × 5

21) 5
    × 7

22) 1
    × 5

23) 5
    × 5

24) 3
    × 5

25) 5
    × 4

26) 3
    × 5

27) 5
    × 7

28) 7
    × 5

29) 5
    × 9

30) 9
    × 5

31) 5
    × 8

32) 9
    × 5

33) 5
    × 8

34) 6
    × 5

35) 5
    × 6

36) 1
    × 5

37) 5
    × 7

38) 7
    × 5

39) 5
    × 4

40) 8
    × 5

41) 5
    × 6

42) 0
    × 5

43) 5
    × 8

44) 5
    × 5

45) 5
    × 9

46) 1
    × 5

47) 5
    × 1

48) 0
    × 5

49) 5
    × 2

50) 7
    × 5

51) 5
    × 2

52) 5
    × 5

53) 5
    × 7

54) 7
    × 5

55) 5
    × 0

56) 5
    × 5

57) 5
    × 3

58) 0
    × 5

59) 5
    × 8

60) 5
    × 5

Let's Multiply 5

1)   5
   × 0

2)   3
   × 5

3)   5
   × 6

4)   6
   × 5

5)   5
   × 0

6)   0
   × 5

7)   5
   × 0

8)   6
   × 5

9)   5
   × 7

10)   9
    × 5

11)   5
    × 3

12)   6
    × 5

13)   5
    × 4

14)   9
    × 5

15)   5
    × 4

16)   1
    × 5

17)   5
    × 1

18)   3
    × 5

19)   5
    × 9

20)   8
    × 5

21)   5
    × 3

22)   6
    × 5

23)   5
    × 2

24)   3
    × 5

25)   5
    × 0

26)   8
    × 5

27)   5
    × 8

28)   7
    × 5

29)   5
    × 4

30)   4
    × 5

31)   5
    × 7

32)   7
    × 5

33)   5
    × 0

34)   7
    × 5

35)   5
    × 0

36)   6
    × 5

37)   5
    × 9

38)   2
    × 5

39)   5
    × 1

40)   6
    × 5

41)   5
    × 7

42)   5
    × 5

43)   5
    × 7

44)   0
    × 5

45)   5
    × 4

46)   3
    × 5

47)   5
    × 1

48)   1
    × 5

49)   5
    × 3

50)   0
    × 5

51)   5
    × 1

52)   2
    × 5

53)   5
    × 2

54)   7
    × 5

55)   5
    × 1

56)   0
    × 5

57)   5
    × 5

58)   0
    × 5

59)   5
    × 4

60)   8
    × 5

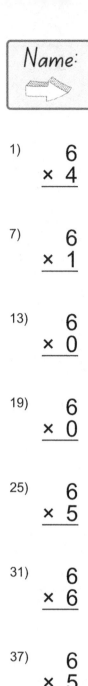 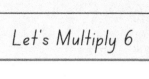
1) 6
    × 4

2) 5
    × 6

3) 6
    × 5

4) 8
    × 6

5) 6
    × 8

6) 1
    × 6

7) 6
    × 1

8) 1
    × 6

9) 6
    × 6

10) 0
    × 6

11) 6
    × 3

12) 1
    × 6

13) 6
    × 0

14) 0
    × 6

15) 6
    × 0

16) 0
    × 6

17) 6
    × 2

18) 7
    × 6

19) 6
    × 0

20) 4
    × 6

21) 6
    × 2

22) 4
    × 6

23) 6
    × 2

24) 7
    × 6

25) 6
    × 5

26) 1
    × 6

27) 6
    × 0

28) 2
    × 6

29) 6
    × 0

30) 6
    × 6

31) 6
    × 6

32) 5
    × 6

33) 6
    × 1

34) 2
    × 6

35) 6
    × 1

36) 1
    × 6

37) 6
    × 5

38) 8
    × 6

39) 6
    × 5

40) 7
    × 6

41) 6
    × 3

42) 8
    × 6

43) 6
    × 7

44) 2
    × 6

45) 6
    × 3

46) 4
    × 6

47) 6
    × 4

48) 6
    × 6

49) 6
    × 4

50) 0
    × 6

51) 6
    × 6

52) 5
    × 6

53) 6
    × 5

54) 9
    × 6

55) 6
    × 6

56) 9
    × 6

57) 6
    × 0

58) 2
    × 6

59) 6
    × 4

60) 4
    × 6

1) 6 × 0

2) 2 × 6

3) 6 × 7

4) 9 × 6

5) 6 × 1

6) 4 × 6

7) 6 × 4

8) 7 × 6

9) 6 × 4

10) 1 × 6

11) 6 × 4

12) 9 × 6

13) 6 × 4

14) 1 × 6

15) 6 × 4

16) 1 × 6

17) 6 × 2

18) 9 × 6

19) 6 × 3

20) 4 × 6

21) 6 × 5

22) 1 × 6

23) 6 × 9

24) 4 × 6

25) 6 × 0

26) 1 × 6

27) 6 × 3

28) 9 × 6

29) 6 × 6

30) 0 × 6

31) 6 × 3

32) 0 × 6

33) 6 × 8

34) 5 × 6

35) 6 × 5

36) 8 × 6

37) 6 × 2

38) 6 × 6

39) 6 × 6

40) 1 × 6

41) 6 × 8

42) 1 × 6

43) 6 × 4

44) 2 × 6

45) 6 × 9

46) 6 × 6

47) 6 × 0

48) 7 × 6

49) 6 × 5

50) 0 × 6

51) 6 × 7

52) 2 × 6

53) 6 × 8

54) 7 × 6

55) 6 × 9

56) 0 × 6

57) 6 × 2

58) 6 × 6

59) 6 × 7

60) 4 × 6

1) 6 × 2

2) 5 × 6

3) 6 × 3

4) 9 × 6

5) 6 × 8

6) 8 × 6

7) 6 × 9

8) 8 × 6

9) 6 × 9

10) 4 × 6

11) 6 × 0

12) 1 × 6

13) 6 × 3

14) 5 × 6

15) 6 × 3

16) 1 × 6

17) 6 × 4

18) 2 × 6

19) 6 × 4

20) 4 × 6

21) 6 × 7

22) 5 × 6

23) 6 × 6

24) 7 × 6

25) 6 × 5

26) 5 × 6

27) 6 × 2

28) 5 × 6

29) 6 × 9

30) 6 × 6

31) 6 × 7

32) 6 × 6

33) 6 × 8

34) 5 × 6

35) 6 × 8

36) 7 × 6

37) 6 × 6

38) 5 × 6

39) 6 × 7

40) 2 × 6

41) 6 × 2

42) 3 × 6

43) 6 × 7

44) 8 × 6

45) 6 × 6

46) 3 × 6

47) 6 × 4

48) 8 × 6

49) 6 × 0

50) 2 × 6

51) 6 × 2

52) 5 × 6

53) 6 × 5

54) 0 × 6

55) 6 × 4

56) 3 × 6

57) 6 × 1

58) 1 × 6

59) 6 × 7

60) 9 × 6

1) $\begin{array}{r} 6 \\ \times\ 7 \\ \hline \end{array}$
2) $\begin{array}{r} 8 \\ \times\ 6 \\ \hline \end{array}$
3) $\begin{array}{r} 6 \\ \times\ 2 \\ \hline \end{array}$
4) $\begin{array}{r} 6 \\ \times\ 6 \\ \hline \end{array}$
5) $\begin{array}{r} 6 \\ \times\ 1 \\ \hline \end{array}$
6) $\begin{array}{r} 4 \\ \times\ 6 \\ \hline \end{array}$

7) $\begin{array}{r} 6 \\ \times\ 5 \\ \hline \end{array}$
8) $\begin{array}{r} 1 \\ \times\ 6 \\ \hline \end{array}$
9) $\begin{array}{r} 6 \\ \times\ 1 \\ \hline \end{array}$
10) $\begin{array}{r} 5 \\ \times\ 6 \\ \hline \end{array}$
11) $\begin{array}{r} 6 \\ \times\ 6 \\ \hline \end{array}$
12) $\begin{array}{r} 7 \\ \times\ 6 \\ \hline \end{array}$

13) $\begin{array}{r} 6 \\ \times\ 4 \\ \hline \end{array}$
14) $\begin{array}{r} 0 \\ \times\ 6 \\ \hline \end{array}$
15) $\begin{array}{r} 6 \\ \times\ 5 \\ \hline \end{array}$
16) $\begin{array}{r} 2 \\ \times\ 6 \\ \hline \end{array}$
17) $\begin{array}{r} 6 \\ \times\ 4 \\ \hline \end{array}$
18) $\begin{array}{r} 5 \\ \times\ 6 \\ \hline \end{array}$

19) $\begin{array}{r} 6 \\ \times\ 2 \\ \hline \end{array}$
20) $\begin{array}{r} 2 \\ \times\ 6 \\ \hline \end{array}$
21) $\begin{array}{r} 6 \\ \times\ 4 \\ \hline \end{array}$
22) $\begin{array}{r} 1 \\ \times\ 6 \\ \hline \end{array}$
23) $\begin{array}{r} 6 \\ \times\ 1 \\ \hline \end{array}$
24) $\begin{array}{r} 0 \\ \times\ 6 \\ \hline \end{array}$

25) $\begin{array}{r} 6 \\ \times\ 0 \\ \hline \end{array}$
26) $\begin{array}{r} 4 \\ \times\ 6 \\ \hline \end{array}$
27) $\begin{array}{r} 6 \\ \times\ 4 \\ \hline \end{array}$
28) $\begin{array}{r} 4 \\ \times\ 6 \\ \hline \end{array}$
29) $\begin{array}{r} 6 \\ \times\ 4 \\ \hline \end{array}$
30) $\begin{array}{r} 5 \\ \times\ 6 \\ \hline \end{array}$

31) $\begin{array}{r} 6 \\ \times\ 6 \\ \hline \end{array}$
32) $\begin{array}{r} 4 \\ \times\ 6 \\ \hline \end{array}$
33) $\begin{array}{r} 6 \\ \times\ 9 \\ \hline \end{array}$
34) $\begin{array}{r} 6 \\ \times\ 6 \\ \hline \end{array}$
35) $\begin{array}{r} 6 \\ \times\ 0 \\ \hline \end{array}$
36) $\begin{array}{r} 4 \\ \times\ 6 \\ \hline \end{array}$

37) $\begin{array}{r} 6 \\ \times\ 3 \\ \hline \end{array}$
38) $\begin{array}{r} 3 \\ \times\ 6 \\ \hline \end{array}$
39) $\begin{array}{r} 6 \\ \times\ 3 \\ \hline \end{array}$
40) $\begin{array}{r} 2 \\ \times\ 6 \\ \hline \end{array}$
41) $\begin{array}{r} 6 \\ \times\ 0 \\ \hline \end{array}$
42) $\begin{array}{r} 7 \\ \times\ 6 \\ \hline \end{array}$

43) $\begin{array}{r} 6 \\ \times\ 7 \\ \hline \end{array}$
44) $\begin{array}{r} 9 \\ \times\ 6 \\ \hline \end{array}$
45) $\begin{array}{r} 6 \\ \times\ 2 \\ \hline \end{array}$
46) $\begin{array}{r} 7 \\ \times\ 6 \\ \hline \end{array}$
47) $\begin{array}{r} 6 \\ \times\ 7 \\ \hline \end{array}$
48) $\begin{array}{r} 1 \\ \times\ 6 \\ \hline \end{array}$

49) $\begin{array}{r} 6 \\ \times\ 6 \\ \hline \end{array}$
50) $\begin{array}{r} 3 \\ \times\ 6 \\ \hline \end{array}$
51) $\begin{array}{r} 6 \\ \times\ 7 \\ \hline \end{array}$
52) $\begin{array}{r} 7 \\ \times\ 6 \\ \hline \end{array}$
53) $\begin{array}{r} 6 \\ \times\ 3 \\ \hline \end{array}$
54) $\begin{array}{r} 9 \\ \times\ 6 \\ \hline \end{array}$

55) $\begin{array}{r} 6 \\ \times\ 5 \\ \hline \end{array}$
56) $\begin{array}{r} 4 \\ \times\ 6 \\ \hline \end{array}$
57) $\begin{array}{r} 6 \\ \times\ 4 \\ \hline \end{array}$
58) $\begin{array}{r} 5 \\ \times\ 6 \\ \hline \end{array}$
59) $\begin{array}{r} 6 \\ \times\ 1 \\ \hline \end{array}$
60) $\begin{array}{r} 5 \\ \times\ 6 \\ \hline \end{array}$

Let's Multiply 6

Time: ———————

1) $\begin{array}{r} 6 \\ \times\ 2 \\ \hline \end{array}$
2) $\begin{array}{r} 6 \\ \times\ 6 \\ \hline \end{array}$
3) $\begin{array}{r} 6 \\ \times\ 8 \\ \hline \end{array}$
4) $\begin{array}{r} 6 \\ \times\ 6 \\ \hline \end{array}$
5) $\begin{array}{r} 6 \\ \times\ 7 \\ \hline \end{array}$
6) $\begin{array}{r} 3 \\ \times\ 6 \\ \hline \end{array}$

7) $\begin{array}{r} 6 \\ \times\ 4 \\ \hline \end{array}$
8) $\begin{array}{r} 9 \\ \times\ 6 \\ \hline \end{array}$
9) $\begin{array}{r} 6 \\ \times\ 0 \\ \hline \end{array}$
10) $\begin{array}{r} 0 \\ \times\ 6 \\ \hline \end{array}$
11) $\begin{array}{r} 6 \\ \times\ 6 \\ \hline \end{array}$
12) $\begin{array}{r} 9 \\ \times\ 6 \\ \hline \end{array}$

13) $\begin{array}{r} 6 \\ \times\ 5 \\ \hline \end{array}$
14) $\begin{array}{r} 5 \\ \times\ 6 \\ \hline \end{array}$
15) $\begin{array}{r} 6 \\ \times\ 3 \\ \hline \end{array}$
16) $\begin{array}{r} 7 \\ \times\ 6 \\ \hline \end{array}$
17) $\begin{array}{r} 6 \\ \times\ 9 \\ \hline \end{array}$
18) $\begin{array}{r} 6 \\ \times\ 6 \\ \hline \end{array}$

19) $\begin{array}{r} 6 \\ \times\ 1 \\ \hline \end{array}$
20) $\begin{array}{r} 9 \\ \times\ 6 \\ \hline \end{array}$
21) $\begin{array}{r} 6 \\ \times\ 7 \\ \hline \end{array}$
22) $\begin{array}{r} 5 \\ \times\ 6 \\ \hline \end{array}$
23) $\begin{array}{r} 6 \\ \times\ 4 \\ \hline \end{array}$
24) $\begin{array}{r} 6 \\ \times\ 6 \\ \hline \end{array}$

25) $\begin{array}{r} 6 \\ \times\ 4 \\ \hline \end{array}$
26) $\begin{array}{r} 0 \\ \times\ 6 \\ \hline \end{array}$
27) $\begin{array}{r} 6 \\ \times\ 8 \\ \hline \end{array}$
28) $\begin{array}{r} 6 \\ \times\ 6 \\ \hline \end{array}$
29) $\begin{array}{r} 6 \\ \times\ 3 \\ \hline \end{array}$
30) $\begin{array}{r} 7 \\ \times\ 6 \\ \hline \end{array}$

31) $\begin{array}{r} 6 \\ \times\ 0 \\ \hline \end{array}$
32) $\begin{array}{r} 6 \\ \times\ 6 \\ \hline \end{array}$
33) $\begin{array}{r} 6 \\ \times\ 3 \\ \hline \end{array}$
34) $\begin{array}{r} 6 \\ \times\ 6 \\ \hline \end{array}$
35) $\begin{array}{r} 6 \\ \times\ 8 \\ \hline \end{array}$
36) $\begin{array}{r} 6 \\ \times\ 6 \\ \hline \end{array}$

37) $\begin{array}{r} 6 \\ \times\ 0 \\ \hline \end{array}$
38) $\begin{array}{r} 3 \\ \times\ 6 \\ \hline \end{array}$
39) $\begin{array}{r} 6 \\ \times\ 5 \\ \hline \end{array}$
40) $\begin{array}{r} 9 \\ \times\ 6 \\ \hline \end{array}$
41) $\begin{array}{r} 6 \\ \times\ 6 \\ \hline \end{array}$
42) $\begin{array}{r} 9 \\ \times\ 6 \\ \hline \end{array}$

43) $\begin{array}{r} 6 \\ \times\ 2 \\ \hline \end{array}$
44) $\begin{array}{r} 3 \\ \times\ 6 \\ \hline \end{array}$
45) $\begin{array}{r} 6 \\ \times\ 9 \\ \hline \end{array}$
46) $\begin{array}{r} 4 \\ \times\ 6 \\ \hline \end{array}$
47) $\begin{array}{r} 6 \\ \times\ 9 \\ \hline \end{array}$
48) $\begin{array}{r} 7 \\ \times\ 6 \\ \hline \end{array}$

49) $\begin{array}{r} 6 \\ \times\ 1 \\ \hline \end{array}$
50) $\begin{array}{r} 6 \\ \times\ 6 \\ \hline \end{array}$
51) $\begin{array}{r} 6 \\ \times\ 1 \\ \hline \end{array}$
52) $\begin{array}{r} 9 \\ \times\ 6 \\ \hline \end{array}$
53) $\begin{array}{r} 6 \\ \times\ 8 \\ \hline \end{array}$
54) $\begin{array}{r} 6 \\ \times\ 6 \\ \hline \end{array}$

55) $\begin{array}{r} 6 \\ \times\ 9 \\ \hline \end{array}$
56) $\begin{array}{r} 0 \\ \times\ 6 \\ \hline \end{array}$
57) $\begin{array}{r} 6 \\ \times\ 7 \\ \hline \end{array}$
58) $\begin{array}{r} 9 \\ \times\ 6 \\ \hline \end{array}$
59) $\begin{array}{r} 6 \\ \times\ 4 \\ \hline \end{array}$
60) $\begin{array}{r} 5 \\ \times\ 6 \\ \hline \end{array}$

Name: _____

Let's Multiply 6

Day
/100

Date: _____
Time: _____

Score
/60

1) 6
  × 0

2) 2
  × 6

3) 6
  × 7

4) 2
  × 6

5) 6
  × 2

6) 6
  × 6

7) 6
  × 8

8) 4
  × 6

9) 6
  × 5

10) 5
  × 6

11) 6
  × 7

12) 1
  × 6

13) 6
  × 5

14) 6
  × 6

15) 6
  × 8

16) 6
  × 6

17) 6
  × 2

18) 2
  × 6

19) 6
  × 2

20) 6
  × 6

21) 6
  × 7

22) 6
  × 6

23) 6
  × 8

24) 6
  × 6

25) 6
  × 7

26) 6
  × 6

27) 6
  × 3

28) 3
  × 6

29) 6
  × 4

30) 7
  × 6

31) 6
  × 8

32) 1
  × 6

33) 6
  × 3

34) 8
  × 6

35) 6
  × 3

36) 8
  × 6

37) 6
  × 7

38) 5
  × 6

39) 6
  × 2

40) 7
  × 6

41) 6
  × 0

42) 4
  × 6

43) 6
  × 0

44) 8
  × 6

45) 6
  × 4

46) 9
  × 6

47) 6
  × 8

48) 0
  × 6

49) 6
  × 7

50) 0
  × 6

51) 6
  × 1

52) 1
  × 6

53) 6
  × 5

54) 8
  × 6

55) 6
  × 9

56) 1
  × 6

57) 6
  × 8

58) 1
  × 6

59) 6
  × 6

60) 5
  × 6

Let's Multiply 6

1) $\begin{array}{r} 6 \\ \times\ 0 \\ \hline \end{array}$	2) $\begin{array}{r} 1 \\ \times\ 6 \\ \hline \end{array}$	3) $\begin{array}{r} 6 \\ \times\ 6 \\ \hline \end{array}$	4) $\begin{array}{r} 8 \\ \times\ 6 \\ \hline \end{array}$	5) $\begin{array}{r} 6 \\ \times\ 9 \\ \hline \end{array}$	6) $\begin{array}{r} 3 \\ \times\ 6 \\ \hline \end{array}$
7) $\begin{array}{r} 6 \\ \times\ 3 \\ \hline \end{array}$	8) $\begin{array}{r} 2 \\ \times\ 6 \\ \hline \end{array}$	9) $\begin{array}{r} 6 \\ \times\ 8 \\ \hline \end{array}$	10) $\begin{array}{r} 5 \\ \times\ 6 \\ \hline \end{array}$	11) $\begin{array}{r} 6 \\ \times\ 6 \\ \hline \end{array}$	12) $\begin{array}{r} 2 \\ \times\ 6 \\ \hline \end{array}$
13) $\begin{array}{r} 6 \\ \times\ 3 \\ \hline \end{array}$	14) $\begin{array}{r} 1 \\ \times\ 6 \\ \hline \end{array}$	15) $\begin{array}{r} 6 \\ \times\ 0 \\ \hline \end{array}$	16) $\begin{array}{r} 8 \\ \times\ 6 \\ \hline \end{array}$	17) $\begin{array}{r} 6 \\ \times\ 1 \\ \hline \end{array}$	18) $\begin{array}{r} 9 \\ \times\ 6 \\ \hline \end{array}$
19) $\begin{array}{r} 6 \\ \times\ 9 \\ \hline \end{array}$	20) $\begin{array}{r} 7 \\ \times\ 6 \\ \hline \end{array}$	21) $\begin{array}{r} 6 \\ \times\ 3 \\ \hline \end{array}$	22) $\begin{array}{r} 8 \\ \times\ 6 \\ \hline \end{array}$	23) $\begin{array}{r} 6 \\ \times\ 7 \\ \hline \end{array}$	24) $\begin{array}{r} 7 \\ \times\ 6 \\ \hline \end{array}$
25) $\begin{array}{r} 6 \\ \times\ 6 \\ \hline \end{array}$	26) $\begin{array}{r} 6 \\ \times\ 6 \\ \hline \end{array}$	27) $\begin{array}{r} 6 \\ \times\ 5 \\ \hline \end{array}$	28) $\begin{array}{r} 8 \\ \times\ 6 \\ \hline \end{array}$	29) $\begin{array}{r} 6 \\ \times\ 0 \\ \hline \end{array}$	30) $\begin{array}{r} 9 \\ \times\ 6 \\ \hline \end{array}$
31) $\begin{array}{r} 6 \\ \times\ 2 \\ \hline \end{array}$	32) $\begin{array}{r} 5 \\ \times\ 6 \\ \hline \end{array}$	33) $\begin{array}{r} 6 \\ \times\ 9 \\ \hline \end{array}$	34) $\begin{array}{r} 1 \\ \times\ 6 \\ \hline \end{array}$	35) $\begin{array}{r} 6 \\ \times\ 5 \\ \hline \end{array}$	36) $\begin{array}{r} 7 \\ \times\ 6 \\ \hline \end{array}$
37) $\begin{array}{r} 6 \\ \times\ 1 \\ \hline \end{array}$	38) $\begin{array}{r} 9 \\ \times\ 6 \\ \hline \end{array}$	39) $\begin{array}{r} 6 \\ \times\ 8 \\ \hline \end{array}$	40) $\begin{array}{r} 0 \\ \times\ 6 \\ \hline \end{array}$	41) $\begin{array}{r} 6 \\ \times\ 6 \\ \hline \end{array}$	42) $\begin{array}{r} 6 \\ \times\ 6 \\ \hline \end{array}$
43) $\begin{array}{r} 6 \\ \times\ 7 \\ \hline \end{array}$	44) $\begin{array}{r} 5 \\ \times\ 6 \\ \hline \end{array}$	45) $\begin{array}{r} 6 \\ \times\ 6 \\ \hline \end{array}$	46) $\begin{array}{r} 6 \\ \times\ 6 \\ \hline \end{array}$	47) $\begin{array}{r} 6 \\ \times\ 8 \\ \hline \end{array}$	48) $\begin{array}{r} 9 \\ \times\ 6 \\ \hline \end{array}$
49) $\begin{array}{r} 6 \\ \times\ 7 \\ \hline \end{array}$	50) $\begin{array}{r} 1 \\ \times\ 6 \\ \hline \end{array}$	51) $\begin{array}{r} 6 \\ \times\ 6 \\ \hline \end{array}$	52) $\begin{array}{r} 3 \\ \times\ 6 \\ \hline \end{array}$	53) $\begin{array}{r} 6 \\ \times\ 0 \\ \hline \end{array}$	54) $\begin{array}{r} 3 \\ \times\ 6 \\ \hline \end{array}$
55) $\begin{array}{r} 6 \\ \times\ 6 \\ \hline \end{array}$	56) $\begin{array}{r} 4 \\ \times\ 6 \\ \hline \end{array}$	57) $\begin{array}{r} 6 \\ \times\ 2 \\ \hline \end{array}$	58) $\begin{array}{r} 8 \\ \times\ 6 \\ \hline \end{array}$	59) $\begin{array}{r} 6 \\ \times\ 8 \\ \hline \end{array}$	60) $\begin{array}{r} 0 \\ \times\ 6 \\ \hline \end{array}$

Name: _____

Let's Multiply 7

Day /100

Date: _____
Time: _____

Score /60

1) 7
× 8

2) 1
× 7

3) 7
× 3

4) 3
× 7

5) 7
× 8

6) 8
× 7

7) 7
× 5

8) 7
× 7

9) 7
× 4

10) 8
× 7

11) 7
× 7

12) 2
× 7

13) 7
× 2

14) 3
× 7

15) 7
× 3

16) 4
× 7

17) 7
× 8

18) 7
× 7

19) 7
× 1

20) 4
× 7

21) 7
× 8

22) 4
× 7

23) 7
× 6

24) 4
× 7

25) 7
× 0

26) 9
× 7

27) 7
× 9

28) 2
× 7

29) 7
× 1

30) 3
× 7

31) 7
× 4

32) 9
× 7

33) 7
× 7

34) 2
× 7

35) 7
× 3

36) 3
× 7

37) 7
× 6

38) 3
× 7

39) 7
× 6

40) 3
× 7

41) 7
× 2

42) 3
× 7

43) 7
× 1

44) 8
× 7

45) 7
× 7

46) 1
× 7

47) 7
× 9

48) 2
× 7

49) 7
× 8

50) 7
× 7

51) 7
× 8

52) 0
× 7

53) 7
× 1

54) 1
× 7

55) 7
× 3

56) 9
× 7

57) 7
× 4

58) 0
× 7

59) 7
× 5

60) 6
× 7

Name: _____

Let's Multiply 7

Day /100

Date: _____
Time: _____

Score /60

1) 7
   × 3

2) 3
   × 7

3) 7
   × 3

4) 7
   × 7

5) 7
   × 3

6) 6
   × 7

7) 7
   × 1

8) 7
   × 7

9) 7
   × 5

10) 4
    × 7

11) 7
    × 3

12) 5
    × 7

13) 7
    × 9

14) 7
    × 7

15) 7
    × 8

16) 8
    × 7

17) 7
    × 3

18) 8
    × 7

19) 7
    × 4

20) 8
    × 7

21) 7
    × 5

22) 8
    × 7

23) 7
    × 9

24) 3
    × 7

25) 7
    × 9

26) 9
    × 7

27) 7
    × 8

28) 3
    × 7

29) 7
    × 8

30) 8
    × 7

31) 7
    × 7

32) 1
    × 7

33) 7
    × 0

34) 7
    × 7

35) 7
    × 5

36) 1
    × 7

37) 7
    × 9

38) 2
    × 7

39) 7
    × 8

40) 0
    × 7

41) 7
    × 8

42) 4
    × 7

43) 7
    × 1

44) 3
    × 7

45) 7
    × 5

46) 9
    × 7

47) 7
    × 7

48) 6
    × 7

49) 7
    × 6

50) 8
    × 7

51) 7
    × 2

52) 8
    × 7

53) 7
    × 0

54) 9
    × 7

55) 7
    × 3

56) 0
    × 7

57) 7
    × 3

58) 7
    × 7

59) 7
    × 0

60) 7
    × 7

1)　　7
　　× 7

2)　　8
　　× 7

3)　　7
　　× 3

4)　　1
　　× 7

5)　　7
　　× 8

6)　　7
　　× 7

7)　　7
　　× 5

8)　　9
　　× 7

9)　　7
　　× 9

10)　　5
　　× 7

11)　　7
　　× 9

12)　　6
　　× 7

13)　　7
　　× 0

14)　　7
　　× 7

15)　　7
　　× 6

16)　　4
　　× 7

17)　　7
　　× 5

18)　　4
　　× 7

19)　　7
　　× 1

20)　　5
　　× 7

21)　　7
　　× 0

22)　　8
　　× 7

23)　　7
　　× 1

24)　　5
　　× 7

25)　　7
　　× 6

26)　　2
　　× 7

27)　　7
　　× 2

28)　　6
　　× 7

29)　　7
　　× 9

30)　　5
　　× 7

31)　　7
　　× 2

32)　　8
　　× 7

33)　　7
　　× 5

34)　　1
　　× 7

35)　　7
　　× 5

36)　　1
　　× 7

37)　　7
　　× 5

38)　　6
　　× 7

39)　　7
　　× 3

40)　　9
　　× 7

41)　　7
　　× 9

42)　　7
　　× 7

43)　　7
　　× 5

44)　　0
　　× 7

45)　　7
　　× 1

46)　　7
　　× 7

47)　　7
　　× 5

48)　　9
　　× 7

49)　　7
　　× 0

50)　　3
　　× 7

51)　　7
　　× 8

52)　　0
　　× 7

53)　　7
　　× 5

54)　　7
　　× 7

55)　　7
　　× 2

56)　　0
　　× 7

57)　　7
　　× 4

58)　　8
　　× 7

59)　　7
　　× 3

60)　　0
　　× 7

Name: _____

Let's Multiply 7

Day
/100

Date: _____
Time: _____

Score
/60

1) 7
   × 3

2) 8
   × 7

3) 7
   × 7

4) 7
   × 7

5) 7
   × 7

6) 5
   × 7

7) 7
   × 6

8) 7
   × 7

9) 7
   × 3

10) 3
    × 7

11) 7
    × 9

12) 0
    × 7

13) 7
    × 0

14) 3
    × 7

15) 7
    × 3

16) 7
    × 7

17) 7
    × 6

18) 9
    × 7

19) 7
    × 5

20) 2
    × 7

21) 7
    × 6

22) 9
    × 7

23) 7
    × 0

24) 5
    × 7

25) 7
    × 8

26) 9
    × 7

27) 7
    × 2

28) 9
    × 7

29) 7
    × 9

30) 0
    × 7

31) 7
    × 7

32) 9
    × 7

33) 7
    × 1

34) 9
    × 7

35) 7
    × 5

36) 7
    × 7

37) 7
    × 6

38) 7
    × 7

39) 7
    × 2

40) 2
    × 7

41) 7
    × 2

42) 4
    × 7

43) 7
    × 2

44) 1
    × 7

45) 7
    × 5

46) 7
    × 7

47) 7
    × 0

48) 0
    × 7

49) 7
    × 7

50) 1
    × 7

51) 7
    × 2

52) 9
    × 7

53) 7
    × 9

54) 5
    × 7

55) 7
    × 2

56) 3
    × 7

57) 7
    × 9

58) 1
    × 7

59) 7
    × 3

60) 4
    × 7

1) 7
× 0

2) 6
× 7

3) 7
× 5

4) 9
× 7

5) 7
× 9

6) 6
× 7

7) 7
× 0

8) 5
× 7

9) 7
× 3

10) 2
× 7

11) 7
× 5

12) 4
× 7

13) 7
× 5

14) 8
× 7

15) 7
× 6

16) 6
× 7

17) 7
× 0

18) 2
× 7

19) 7
× 8

20) 4
× 7

21) 7
× 8

22) 9
× 7

23) 7
× 0

24) 2
× 7

25) 7
× 7

26) 0
× 7

27) 7
× 3

28) 8
× 7

29) 7
× 8

30) 5
× 7

31) 7
× 0

32) 7
× 7

33) 7
× 4

34) 5
× 7

35) 7
× 2

36) 7
× 7

37) 7
× 3

38) 7
× 7

39) 7
× 0

40) 5
× 7

41) 7
× 1

42) 2
× 7

43) 7
× 2

44) 1
× 7

45) 7
× 8

46) 2
× 7

47) 7
× 5

48) 9
× 7

49) 7
× 0

50) 8
× 7

51) 7
× 5

52) 2
× 7

53) 7
× 0

54) 2
× 7

55) 7
× 6

56) 7
× 7

57) 7
× 6

58) 6
× 7

59) 7
× 3

60) 6
× 7

1) 7
   × 6

2) 5
   × 7

3) 7
   × 0

4) 2
   × 7

5) 7
   × 5

6) 6
   × 7

7) 7
   × 8

8) 7
   × 7

9) 7
   × 8

10) 0
    × 7

11) 7
    × 5

12) 3
    × 7

13) 7
    × 2

14) 4
    × 7

15) 7
    × 4

16) 6
    × 7

17) 7
    × 5

18) 3
    × 7

19) 7
    × 3

20) 9
    × 7

21) 7
    × 2

22) 4
    × 7

23) 7
    × 8

24) 4
    × 7

25) 7
    × 8

26) 2
    × 7

27) 7
    × 6

28) 0
    × 7

29) 7
    × 7

30) 1
    × 7

31) 7
    × 6

32) 7
    × 7

33) 7
    × 9

34) 3
    × 7

35) 7
    × 3

36) 3
    × 7

37) 7
    × 9

38) 0
    × 7

39) 7
    × 7

40) 9
    × 7

41) 7
    × 6

42) 9
    × 7

43) 7
    × 3

44) 4
    × 7

45) 7
    × 4

46) 7
    × 7

47) 7
    × 3

48) 3
    × 7

49) 7
    × 6

50) 5
    × 7

51) 7
    × 5

52) 1
    × 7

53) 7
    × 0

54) 2
    × 7

55) 7
    × 2

56) 0
    × 7

57) 7
    × 3

58) 6
    × 7

59) 7
    × 9

60) 7
    × 7

Name: _____

Let's Multiply 7

Day /100

Date: _____
Time: _____

Score /60

1) 7 × 5

2) 5 × 7

3) 7 × 9

4) 0 × 7

5) 7 × 4

6) 1 × 7

7) 7 × 4

8) 5 × 7

9) 7 × 7

10) 3 × 7

11) 7 × 4

12) 1 × 7

13) 7 × 2

14) 7 × 7

15) 7 × 9

16) 9 × 7

17) 7 × 8

18) 6 × 7

19) 7 × 4

20) 9 × 7

21) 7 × 5

22) 0 × 7

23) 7 × 2

24) 7 × 7

25) 7 × 9

26) 8 × 7

27) 7 × 3

28) 5 × 7

29) 7 × 3

30) 8 × 7

31) 7 × 9

32) 6 × 7

33) 7 × 0

34) 3 × 7

35) 7 × 3

36) 0 × 7

37) 7 × 8

38) 5 × 7

39) 7 × 0

40) 4 × 7

41) 7 × 2

42) 1 × 7

43) 7 × 1

44) 7 × 7

45) 7 × 3

46) 7 × 7

47) 7 × 5

48) 3 × 7

49) 7 × 8

50) 5 × 7

51) 7 × 4

52) 5 × 7

53) 7 × 5

54) 5 × 7

55) 7 × 6

56) 0 × 7

57) 7 × 9

58) 9 × 7

59) 7 × 0

60) 9 × 7

Name: _____

Let's Multiply 8

Day /100

Date: _____
Time: _____

Score /60

1)   8
   × 4

2)   3
   × 8

3)   8
   × 6

4)   3
   × 8

5)   8
   × 3

6)   1
   × 8

7)   8
   × 8

8)   0
   × 8

9)   8
   × 3

10)   6
    × 8

11)   8
    × 6

12)   5
    × 8

13)   8
    × 5

14)   2
    × 8

15)   8
    × 5

16)   2
    × 8

17)   8
    × 0

18)   1
    × 8

19)   8
    × 7

20)   7
    × 8

21)   8
    × 9

22)   8
    × 8

23)   8
    × 1

24)   6
    × 8

25)   8
    × 0

26)   5
    × 8

27)   8
    × 3

28)   1
    × 8

29)   8
    × 3

30)   6
    × 8

31)   8
    × 1

32)   3
    × 8

33)   8
    × 4

34)   5
    × 8

35)   8
    × 9

36)   0
    × 8

37)   8
    × 7

38)   8
    × 8

39)   8
    × 5

40)   0
    × 8

41)   8
    × 5

42)   0
    × 8

43)   8
    × 3

44)   3
    × 8

45)   8
    × 2

46)   4
    × 8

47)   8
    × 3

48)   7
    × 8

49)   8
    × 2

50)   0
    × 8

51)   8
    × 3

52)   6
    × 8

53)   8
    × 6

54)   3
    × 8

55)   8
    × 2

56)   4
    × 8

57)   8
    × 4

58)   5
    × 8

59)   8
    × 5

60)   6
    × 8

Name: _____

Let's Multiply 8

Day /100

Date: _____

Time: _____

Score /60

1)
$$\begin{array}{r} 8 \\ \times\ 1 \\ \hline \end{array}$$

2)
$$\begin{array}{r} 8 \\ \times\ 8 \\ \hline \end{array}$$

3)
$$\begin{array}{r} 8 \\ \times\ 5 \\ \hline \end{array}$$

4)
$$\begin{array}{r} 4 \\ \times\ 8 \\ \hline \end{array}$$

5)
$$\begin{array}{r} 8 \\ \times\ 1 \\ \hline \end{array}$$

6)
$$\begin{array}{r} 3 \\ \times\ 8 \\ \hline \end{array}$$

7)
$$\begin{array}{r} 8 \\ \times\ 1 \\ \hline \end{array}$$

8)
$$\begin{array}{r} 5 \\ \times\ 8 \\ \hline \end{array}$$

9)
$$\begin{array}{r} 8 \\ \times\ 5 \\ \hline \end{array}$$

10)
$$\begin{array}{r} 2 \\ \times\ 8 \\ \hline \end{array}$$

11)
$$\begin{array}{r} 8 \\ \times\ 7 \\ \hline \end{array}$$

12)
$$\begin{array}{r} 9 \\ \times\ 8 \\ \hline \end{array}$$

13)
$$\begin{array}{r} 8 \\ \times\ 5 \\ \hline \end{array}$$

14)
$$\begin{array}{r} 2 \\ \times\ 8 \\ \hline \end{array}$$

15)
$$\begin{array}{r} 8 \\ \times\ 5 \\ \hline \end{array}$$

16)
$$\begin{array}{r} 9 \\ \times\ 8 \\ \hline \end{array}$$

17)
$$\begin{array}{r} 8 \\ \times\ 3 \\ \hline \end{array}$$

18)
$$\begin{array}{r} 1 \\ \times\ 8 \\ \hline \end{array}$$

19)
$$\begin{array}{r} 8 \\ \times\ 2 \\ \hline \end{array}$$

20)
$$\begin{array}{r} 4 \\ \times\ 8 \\ \hline \end{array}$$

21)
$$\begin{array}{r} 8 \\ \times\ 7 \\ \hline \end{array}$$

22)
$$\begin{array}{r} 6 \\ \times\ 8 \\ \hline \end{array}$$

23)
$$\begin{array}{r} 8 \\ \times\ 2 \\ \hline \end{array}$$

24)
$$\begin{array}{r} 4 \\ \times\ 8 \\ \hline \end{array}$$

25)
$$\begin{array}{r} 8 \\ \times\ 2 \\ \hline \end{array}$$

26)
$$\begin{array}{r} 8 \\ \times\ 8 \\ \hline \end{array}$$

27)
$$\begin{array}{r} 8 \\ \times\ 5 \\ \hline \end{array}$$

28)
$$\begin{array}{r} 2 \\ \times\ 8 \\ \hline \end{array}$$

29)
$$\begin{array}{r} 8 \\ \times\ 9 \\ \hline \end{array}$$

30)
$$\begin{array}{r} 9 \\ \times\ 8 \\ \hline \end{array}$$

31)
$$\begin{array}{r} 8 \\ \times\ 9 \\ \hline \end{array}$$

32)
$$\begin{array}{r} 1 \\ \times\ 8 \\ \hline \end{array}$$

33)
$$\begin{array}{r} 8 \\ \times\ 2 \\ \hline \end{array}$$

34)
$$\begin{array}{r} 5 \\ \times\ 8 \\ \hline \end{array}$$

35)
$$\begin{array}{r} 8 \\ \times\ 4 \\ \hline \end{array}$$

36)
$$\begin{array}{r} 0 \\ \times\ 8 \\ \hline \end{array}$$

37)
$$\begin{array}{r} 8 \\ \times\ 0 \\ \hline \end{array}$$

38)
$$\begin{array}{r} 5 \\ \times\ 8 \\ \hline \end{array}$$

39)
$$\begin{array}{r} 8 \\ \times\ 8 \\ \hline \end{array}$$

40)
$$\begin{array}{r} 2 \\ \times\ 8 \\ \hline \end{array}$$

41)
$$\begin{array}{r} 8 \\ \times\ 4 \\ \hline \end{array}$$

42)
$$\begin{array}{r} 8 \\ \times\ 8 \\ \hline \end{array}$$

43)
$$\begin{array}{r} 8 \\ \times\ 8 \\ \hline \end{array}$$

44)
$$\begin{array}{r} 3 \\ \times\ 8 \\ \hline \end{array}$$

45)
$$\begin{array}{r} 8 \\ \times\ 9 \\ \hline \end{array}$$

46)
$$\begin{array}{r} 7 \\ \times\ 8 \\ \hline \end{array}$$

47)
$$\begin{array}{r} 8 \\ \times\ 1 \\ \hline \end{array}$$

48)
$$\begin{array}{r} 0 \\ \times\ 8 \\ \hline \end{array}$$

49)
$$\begin{array}{r} 8 \\ \times\ 8 \\ \hline \end{array}$$

50)
$$\begin{array}{r} 9 \\ \times\ 8 \\ \hline \end{array}$$

51)
$$\begin{array}{r} 8 \\ \times\ 4 \\ \hline \end{array}$$

52)
$$\begin{array}{r} 8 \\ \times\ 8 \\ \hline \end{array}$$

53)
$$\begin{array}{r} 8 \\ \times\ 4 \\ \hline \end{array}$$

54)
$$\begin{array}{r} 4 \\ \times\ 8 \\ \hline \end{array}$$

55)
$$\begin{array}{r} 8 \\ \times\ 5 \\ \hline \end{array}$$

56)
$$\begin{array}{r} 8 \\ \times\ 8 \\ \hline \end{array}$$

57)
$$\begin{array}{r} 8 \\ \times\ 9 \\ \hline \end{array}$$

58)
$$\begin{array}{r} 7 \\ \times\ 8 \\ \hline \end{array}$$

59)
$$\begin{array}{r} 8 \\ \times\ 2 \\ \hline \end{array}$$

60)
$$\begin{array}{r} 4 \\ \times\ 8 \\ \hline \end{array}$$

Name: _____

Let's Multiply 8

Day /100

Date: _____

Time: _____

Score /60

1) 8 × 4

2) 1 × 8

3) 8 × 6

4) 3 × 8

5) 8 × 3

6) 3 × 8

7) 8 × 8

8) 9 × 8

9) 8 × 2

10) 9 × 8

11) 8 × 5

12) 1 × 8

13) 8 × 7

14) 5 × 8

15) 8 × 5

16) 8 × 8

17) 8 × 3

18) 5 × 8

19) 8 × 7

20) 1 × 8

21) 8 × 8

22) 4 × 8

23) 8 × 6

24) 2 × 8

25) 8 × 5

26) 9 × 8

27) 8 × 5

28) 5 × 8

29) 8 × 6

30) 1 × 8

31) 8 × 7

32) 6 × 8

33) 8 × 2

34) 0 × 8

35) 8 × 2

36) 2 × 8

37) 8 × 0

38) 2 × 8

39) 8 × 2

40) 1 × 8

41) 8 × 1

42) 1 × 8

43) 8 × 4

44) 7 × 8

45) 8 × 0

46) 4 × 8

47) 8 × 1

48) 7 × 8

49) 8 × 3

50) 5 × 8

51) 8 × 3

52) 2 × 8

53) 8 × 9

54) 0 × 8

55) 8 × 9

56) 9 × 8

57) 8 × 5

58) 9 × 8

59) 8 × 3

60) 5 × 8

Name: _____

Let's Multiply 8

Day /100

Date: _____
Time: _____

Score /60

1) 8
  × 6

2) 3
  × 8

3) 8
  × 6

4) 4
  × 8

5) 8
  × 3

6) 4
  × 8

7) 8
  × 8

8) 5
  × 8

9) 8
  × 8

10) 0
   × 8

11) 8
   × 8

12) 2
   × 8

13) 8
   × 0

14) 5
   × 8

15) 8
   × 9

16) 1
   × 8

17) 8
   × 7

18) 1
   × 8

19) 8
   × 0

20) 4
   × 8

21) 8
   × 7

22) 8
   × 8

23) 8
   × 9

24) 8
   × 8

25) 8
   × 6

26) 7
   × 8

27) 8
   × 1

28) 5
   × 8

29) 8
   × 2

30) 2
   × 8

31) 8
   × 1

32) 4
   × 8

33) 8
   × 9

34) 9
   × 8

35) 8
   × 3

36) 0
   × 8

37) 8
   × 5

38) 1
   × 8

39) 8
   × 9

40) 8
   × 8

41) 8
   × 2

42) 6
   × 8

43) 8
   × 2

44) 1
   × 8

45) 8
   × 1

46) 0
   × 8

47) 8
   × 5

48) 3
   × 8

49) 8
   × 7

50) 9
   × 8

51) 8
   × 3

52) 0
   × 8

53) 8
   × 2

54) 8
   × 8

55) 8
   × 6

56) 5
   × 8

57) 8
   × 6

58) 6
   × 8

59) 8
   × 3

60) 7
   × 8

Let's Multiply 8

1)   8
   × 4

2)   2
   × 8

3)   8
   × 4

4)   7
   × 8

5)   8
   × 3

6)   7
   × 8

7)   8
   × 1

8)   2
   × 8

9)   8
   × 9

10)   1
   × 8

11)   8
   × 0

12)   3
   × 8

13)   8
   × 2

14)   1
   × 8

15)   8
   × 0

16)   1
   × 8

17)   8
   × 2

18)   9
   × 8

19)   8
   × 4

20)   4
   × 8

21)   8
   × 3

22)   1
   × 8

23)   8
   × 4

24)   9
   × 8

25)   8
   × 9

26)   1
   × 8

27)   8
   × 1

28)   6
   × 8

29)   8
   × 6

30)   9
   × 8

31)   8
   × 8

32)   0
   × 8

33)   8
   × 6

34)   6
   × 8

35)   8
   × 5

36)   7
   × 8

37)   8
   × 9

38)   6
   × 8

39)   8
   × 6

40)   6
   × 8

41)   8
   × 8

42)   0
   × 8

43)   8
   × 9

44)   7
   × 8

45)   8
   × 0

46)   0
   × 8

47)   8
   × 2

48)   7
   × 8

49)   8
   × 1

50)   0
   × 8

51)   8
   × 2

52)   7
   × 8

53)   8
   × 5

54)   4
   × 8

55)   8
   × 6

56)   3
   × 8

57)   8
   × 3

58)   4
   × 8

59)   8
   × 4

60)   7
   × 8

Name: _____

Let's Multiply 8

Day /100

Date: _____
Time: _____

Score /60

1) 8
  × 5

2) 9
  × 8

3) 8
  × 1

4) 9
  × 8

5) 8
  × 2

6) 8
  × 8

7) 8
  × 5

8) 6
  × 8

9) 8
  × 1

10) 9
   × 8

11) 8
   × 8

12) 6
   × 8

13) 8
   × 5

14) 9
   × 8

15) 8
   × 9

16) 7
   × 8

17) 8
   × 0

18) 9
   × 8

19) 8
   × 6

20) 7
   × 8

21) 8
   × 5

22) 7
   × 8

23) 8
   × 6

24) 4
   × 8

25) 8
   × 0

26) 1
   × 8

27) 8
   × 3

28) 8
   × 8

29) 8
   × 9

30) 5
   × 8

31) 8
   × 8

32) 4
   × 8

33) 8
   × 2

34) 7
   × 8

35) 8
   × 8

36) 5
   × 8

37) 8
   × 7

38) 7
   × 8

39) 8
   × 6

40) 9
   × 8

41) 8
   × 8

42) 9
   × 8

43) 8
   × 8

44) 7
   × 8

45) 8
   × 3

46) 5
   × 8

47) 8
   × 6

48) 0
   × 8

49) 8
   × 5

50) 3
   × 8

51) 8
   × 1

52) 9
   × 8

53) 8
   × 8

54) 1
   × 8

55) 8
   × 8

56) 1
   × 8

57) 8
   × 4

58) 1
   × 8

59) 8
   × 5

60) 2
   × 8

Name: _____
Let's Multiply 8
Day /100
Date: _____
Time: _____
Score /60

1) $\begin{array}{r} 8 \\ \times\ 0 \\ \hline \end{array}$
2) $\begin{array}{r} 7 \\ \times\ 8 \\ \hline \end{array}$
3) $\begin{array}{r} 8 \\ \times\ 2 \\ \hline \end{array}$
4) $\begin{array}{r} 3 \\ \times\ 8 \\ \hline \end{array}$
5) $\begin{array}{r} 8 \\ \times\ 5 \\ \hline \end{array}$
6) $\begin{array}{r} 6 \\ \times\ 8 \\ \hline \end{array}$

7) $\begin{array}{r} 8 \\ \times\ 4 \\ \hline \end{array}$
8) $\begin{array}{r} 0 \\ \times\ 8 \\ \hline \end{array}$
9) $\begin{array}{r} 8 \\ \times\ 5 \\ \hline \end{array}$
10) $\begin{array}{r} 6 \\ \times\ 8 \\ \hline \end{array}$
11) $\begin{array}{r} 8 \\ \times\ 5 \\ \hline \end{array}$
12) $\begin{array}{r} 9 \\ \times\ 8 \\ \hline \end{array}$

13) $\begin{array}{r} 8 \\ \times\ 5 \\ \hline \end{array}$
14) $\begin{array}{r} 0 \\ \times\ 8 \\ \hline \end{array}$
15) $\begin{array}{r} 8 \\ \times\ 2 \\ \hline \end{array}$
16) $\begin{array}{r} 5 \\ \times\ 8 \\ \hline \end{array}$
17) $\begin{array}{r} 8 \\ \times\ 6 \\ \hline \end{array}$
18) $\begin{array}{r} 2 \\ \times\ 8 \\ \hline \end{array}$

19) $\begin{array}{r} 8 \\ \times\ 7 \\ \hline \end{array}$
20) $\begin{array}{r} 6 \\ \times\ 8 \\ \hline \end{array}$
21) $\begin{array}{r} 8 \\ \times\ 0 \\ \hline \end{array}$
22) $\begin{array}{r} 6 \\ \times\ 8 \\ \hline \end{array}$
23) $\begin{array}{r} 8 \\ \times\ 1 \\ \hline \end{array}$
24) $\begin{array}{r} 6 \\ \times\ 8 \\ \hline \end{array}$

25) $\begin{array}{r} 8 \\ \times\ 7 \\ \hline \end{array}$
26) $\begin{array}{r} 8 \\ \times\ 8 \\ \hline \end{array}$
27) $\begin{array}{r} 8 \\ \times\ 9 \\ \hline \end{array}$
28) $\begin{array}{r} 7 \\ \times\ 8 \\ \hline \end{array}$
29) $\begin{array}{r} 8 \\ \times\ 5 \\ \hline \end{array}$
30) $\begin{array}{r} 9 \\ \times\ 8 \\ \hline \end{array}$

31) $\begin{array}{r} 8 \\ \times\ 9 \\ \hline \end{array}$
32) $\begin{array}{r} 7 \\ \times\ 8 \\ \hline \end{array}$
33) $\begin{array}{r} 8 \\ \times\ 8 \\ \hline \end{array}$
34) $\begin{array}{r} 4 \\ \times\ 8 \\ \hline \end{array}$
35) $\begin{array}{r} 8 \\ \times\ 3 \\ \hline \end{array}$
36) $\begin{array}{r} 9 \\ \times\ 8 \\ \hline \end{array}$

37) $\begin{array}{r} 8 \\ \times\ 6 \\ \hline \end{array}$
38) $\begin{array}{r} 3 \\ \times\ 8 \\ \hline \end{array}$
39) $\begin{array}{r} 8 \\ \times\ 7 \\ \hline \end{array}$
40) $\begin{array}{r} 7 \\ \times\ 8 \\ \hline \end{array}$
41) $\begin{array}{r} 8 \\ \times\ 9 \\ \hline \end{array}$
42) $\begin{array}{r} 4 \\ \times\ 8 \\ \hline \end{array}$

43) $\begin{array}{r} 8 \\ \times\ 6 \\ \hline \end{array}$
44) $\begin{array}{r} 5 \\ \times\ 8 \\ \hline \end{array}$
45) $\begin{array}{r} 8 \\ \times\ 9 \\ \hline \end{array}$
46) $\begin{array}{r} 9 \\ \times\ 8 \\ \hline \end{array}$
47) $\begin{array}{r} 8 \\ \times\ 4 \\ \hline \end{array}$
48) $\begin{array}{r} 5 \\ \times\ 8 \\ \hline \end{array}$

49) $\begin{array}{r} 8 \\ \times\ 1 \\ \hline \end{array}$
50) $\begin{array}{r} 2 \\ \times\ 8 \\ \hline \end{array}$
51) $\begin{array}{r} 8 \\ \times\ 3 \\ \hline \end{array}$
52) $\begin{array}{r} 1 \\ \times\ 8 \\ \hline \end{array}$
53) $\begin{array}{r} 8 \\ \times\ 0 \\ \hline \end{array}$
54) $\begin{array}{r} 2 \\ \times\ 8 \\ \hline \end{array}$

55) $\begin{array}{r} 8 \\ \times\ 6 \\ \hline \end{array}$
56) $\begin{array}{r} 9 \\ \times\ 8 \\ \hline \end{array}$
57) $\begin{array}{r} 8 \\ \times\ 8 \\ \hline \end{array}$
58) $\begin{array}{r} 6 \\ \times\ 8 \\ \hline \end{array}$
59) $\begin{array}{r} 8 \\ \times\ 2 \\ \hline \end{array}$
60) $\begin{array}{r} 9 \\ \times\ 8 \\ \hline \end{array}$

Name: _____

Let's Multiply 9

Day /100

Date: _____

Time: _____

Score /60

1) 9 × 9

2) 4 × 9

3) 9 × 8

4) 2 × 9

5) 9 × 6

6) 2 × 9

7) 9 × 9

8) 4 × 9

9) 9 × 1

10) 9 × 9

11) 9 × 6

12) 0 × 9

13) 9 × 7

14) 2 × 9

15) 9 × 7

16) 3 × 9

17) 9 × 7

18) 7 × 9

19) 9 × 3

20) 4 × 9

21) 9 × 1

22) 5 × 9

23) 9 × 3

24) 4 × 9

25) 9 × 9

26) 7 × 9

27) 9 × 9

28) 9 × 9

29) 9 × 4

30) 8 × 9

31) 9 × 9

32) 7 × 9

33) 9 × 3

34) 1 × 9

35) 9 × 0

36) 8 × 9

37) 9 × 3

38) 9 × 9

39) 9 × 8

40) 1 × 9

41) 9 × 7

42) 4 × 9

43) 9 × 1

44) 7 × 9

45) 9 × 9

46) 0 × 9

47) 9 × 5

48) 8 × 9

49) 9 × 0

50) 5 × 9

51) 9 × 4

52) 4 × 9

53) 9 × 0

54) 3 × 9

55) 9 × 3

56) 3 × 9

57) 9 × 4

58) 2 × 9

59) 9 × 5

60) 7 × 9

Name: _____

Let's Multiply 9

Day
/100

Date: _____
Time: _____

Score
/60

1) 9
  × 0

2) 6
  × 9

3) 9
  × 9

4) 5
  × 9

5) 9
  × 5

6) 2
  × 9

7) 9
  × 6

8) 5
  × 9

9) 9
  × 3

10) 8
   × 9

11) 9
   × 6

12) 9
   × 9

13) 9
   × 8

14) 4
   × 9

15) 9
   × 0

16) 3
   × 9

17) 9
   × 4

18) 8
   × 9

19) 9
   × 5

20) 2
   × 9

21) 9
   × 0

22) 8
   × 9

23) 9
   × 3

24) 0
   × 9

25) 9
   × 0

26) 8
   × 9

27) 9
   × 2

28) 8
   × 9

29) 9
   × 0

30) 2
   × 9

31) 9
   × 7

32) 8
   × 9

33) 9
   × 0

34) 0
   × 9

35) 9
   × 5

36) 8
   × 9

37) 9
   × 8

38) 2
   × 9

39) 9
   × 4

40) 4
   × 9

41) 9
   × 7

42) 6
   × 9

43) 9
   × 4

44) 6
   × 9

45) 9
   × 5

46) 6
   × 9

47) 9
   × 3

48) 7
   × 9

49) 9
   × 0

50) 6
   × 9

51) 9
   × 3

52) 7
   × 9

53) 9
   × 4

54) 0
   × 9

55) 9
   × 7

56) 4
   × 9

57) 9
   × 8

58) 0
   × 9

59) 9
   × 2

60) 4
   × 9

1)
$$\begin{array}{r} 9 \\ \times\ 4 \\ \hline \end{array}$$

2)
$$\begin{array}{r} 8 \\ \times\ 9 \\ \hline \end{array}$$

3)
$$\begin{array}{r} 9 \\ \times\ 3 \\ \hline \end{array}$$

4)
$$\begin{array}{r} 1 \\ \times\ 9 \\ \hline \end{array}$$

5)
$$\begin{array}{r} 9 \\ \times\ 9 \\ \hline \end{array}$$

6)
$$\begin{array}{r} 0 \\ \times\ 9 \\ \hline \end{array}$$

7)
$$\begin{array}{r} 9 \\ \times\ 0 \\ \hline \end{array}$$

8)
$$\begin{array}{r} 5 \\ \times\ 9 \\ \hline \end{array}$$

9)
$$\begin{array}{r} 9 \\ \times\ 8 \\ \hline \end{array}$$

10)
$$\begin{array}{r} 1 \\ \times\ 9 \\ \hline \end{array}$$

11)
$$\begin{array}{r} 9 \\ \times\ 8 \\ \hline \end{array}$$

12)
$$\begin{array}{r} 4 \\ \times\ 9 \\ \hline \end{array}$$

13)
$$\begin{array}{r} 9 \\ \times\ 4 \\ \hline \end{array}$$

14)
$$\begin{array}{r} 8 \\ \times\ 9 \\ \hline \end{array}$$

15)
$$\begin{array}{r} 9 \\ \times\ 9 \\ \hline \end{array}$$

16)
$$\begin{array}{r} 3 \\ \times\ 9 \\ \hline \end{array}$$

17)
$$\begin{array}{r} 9 \\ \times\ 8 \\ \hline \end{array}$$

18)
$$\begin{array}{r} 5 \\ \times\ 9 \\ \hline \end{array}$$

19)
$$\begin{array}{r} 9 \\ \times\ 1 \\ \hline \end{array}$$

20)
$$\begin{array}{r} 1 \\ \times\ 9 \\ \hline \end{array}$$

21)
$$\begin{array}{r} 9 \\ \times\ 5 \\ \hline \end{array}$$

22)
$$\begin{array}{r} 1 \\ \times\ 9 \\ \hline \end{array}$$

23)
$$\begin{array}{r} 9 \\ \times\ 7 \\ \hline \end{array}$$

24)
$$\begin{array}{r} 0 \\ \times\ 9 \\ \hline \end{array}$$

25)
$$\begin{array}{r} 9 \\ \times\ 3 \\ \hline \end{array}$$

26)
$$\begin{array}{r} 5 \\ \times\ 9 \\ \hline \end{array}$$

27)
$$\begin{array}{r} 9 \\ \times\ 6 \\ \hline \end{array}$$

28)
$$\begin{array}{r} 3 \\ \times\ 9 \\ \hline \end{array}$$

29)
$$\begin{array}{r} 9 \\ \times\ 6 \\ \hline \end{array}$$

30)
$$\begin{array}{r} 5 \\ \times\ 9 \\ \hline \end{array}$$

31)
$$\begin{array}{r} 9 \\ \times\ 5 \\ \hline \end{array}$$

32)
$$\begin{array}{r} 0 \\ \times\ 9 \\ \hline \end{array}$$

33)
$$\begin{array}{r} 9 \\ \times\ 3 \\ \hline \end{array}$$

34)
$$\begin{array}{r} 8 \\ \times\ 9 \\ \hline \end{array}$$

35)
$$\begin{array}{r} 9 \\ \times\ 6 \\ \hline \end{array}$$

36)
$$\begin{array}{r} 7 \\ \times\ 9 \\ \hline \end{array}$$

37)
$$\begin{array}{r} 9 \\ \times\ 8 \\ \hline \end{array}$$

38)
$$\begin{array}{r} 5 \\ \times\ 9 \\ \hline \end{array}$$

39)
$$\begin{array}{r} 9 \\ \times\ 5 \\ \hline \end{array}$$

40)
$$\begin{array}{r} 6 \\ \times\ 9 \\ \hline \end{array}$$

41)
$$\begin{array}{r} 9 \\ \times\ 0 \\ \hline \end{array}$$

42)
$$\begin{array}{r} 1 \\ \times\ 9 \\ \hline \end{array}$$

43)
$$\begin{array}{r} 9 \\ \times\ 3 \\ \hline \end{array}$$

44)
$$\begin{array}{r} 3 \\ \times\ 9 \\ \hline \end{array}$$

45)
$$\begin{array}{r} 9 \\ \times\ 8 \\ \hline \end{array}$$

46)
$$\begin{array}{r} 8 \\ \times\ 9 \\ \hline \end{array}$$

47)
$$\begin{array}{r} 9 \\ \times\ 5 \\ \hline \end{array}$$

48)
$$\begin{array}{r} 9 \\ \times\ 9 \\ \hline \end{array}$$

49)
$$\begin{array}{r} 9 \\ \times\ 6 \\ \hline \end{array}$$

50)
$$\begin{array}{r} 0 \\ \times\ 9 \\ \hline \end{array}$$

51)
$$\begin{array}{r} 9 \\ \times\ 0 \\ \hline \end{array}$$

52)
$$\begin{array}{r} 3 \\ \times\ 9 \\ \hline \end{array}$$

53)
$$\begin{array}{r} 9 \\ \times\ 8 \\ \hline \end{array}$$

54)
$$\begin{array}{r} 6 \\ \times\ 9 \\ \hline \end{array}$$

55)
$$\begin{array}{r} 9 \\ \times\ 1 \\ \hline \end{array}$$

56)
$$\begin{array}{r} 8 \\ \times\ 9 \\ \hline \end{array}$$

57)
$$\begin{array}{r} 9 \\ \times\ 3 \\ \hline \end{array}$$

58)
$$\begin{array}{r} 7 \\ \times\ 9 \\ \hline \end{array}$$

59)
$$\begin{array}{r} 9 \\ \times\ 2 \\ \hline \end{array}$$

60)
$$\begin{array}{r} 9 \\ \times\ 9 \\ \hline \end{array}$$

1) 9 × 7

2) 3 × 9

3) 9 × 6

4) 9 × 9

5) 9 × 2

6) 8 × 9

7) 9 × 3

8) 1 × 9

9) 9 × 9

10) 8 × 9

11) 9 × 6

12) 1 × 9

13) 9 × 0

14) 7 × 9

15) 9 × 9

16) 4 × 9

17) 9 × 1

18) 7 × 9

19) 9 × 8

20) 8 × 9

21) 9 × 3

22) 5 × 9

23) 9 × 0

24) 0 × 9

25) 9 × 2

26) 5 × 9

27) 9 × 0

28) 1 × 9

29) 9 × 2

30) 4 × 9

31) 9 × 2

32) 7 × 9

33) 9 × 4

34) 2 × 9

35) 9 × 9

36) 6 × 9

37) 9 × 1

38) 6 × 9

39) 9 × 4

40) 5 × 9

41) 9 × 8

42) 1 × 9

43) 9 × 2

44) 3 × 9

45) 9 × 8

46) 4 × 9

47) 9 × 1

48) 0 × 9

49) 9 × 7

50) 6 × 9

51) 9 × 4

52) 8 × 9

53) 9 × 7

54) 6 × 9

55) 9 × 4

56) 4 × 9

57) 9 × 4

58) 3 × 9

59) 9 × 6

60) 9 × 9

Name: _____

Let's Multiply 9

Day /100

Date: _____

Time: _____

Score /60

1) $\begin{array}{r} 9 \\ \times\ 2 \\ \hline \end{array}$

2) $\begin{array}{r} 9 \\ \times\ 9 \\ \hline \end{array}$

3) $\begin{array}{r} 9 \\ \times\ 4 \\ \hline \end{array}$

4) $\begin{array}{r} 1 \\ \times\ 9 \\ \hline \end{array}$

5) $\begin{array}{r} 9 \\ \times\ 6 \\ \hline \end{array}$

6) $\begin{array}{r} 0 \\ \times\ 9 \\ \hline \end{array}$

7) $\begin{array}{r} 9 \\ \times\ 4 \\ \hline \end{array}$

8) $\begin{array}{r} 3 \\ \times\ 9 \\ \hline \end{array}$

9) $\begin{array}{r} 9 \\ \times\ 5 \\ \hline \end{array}$

10) $\begin{array}{r} 3 \\ \times\ 9 \\ \hline \end{array}$

11) $\begin{array}{r} 9 \\ \times\ 7 \\ \hline \end{array}$

12) $\begin{array}{r} 7 \\ \times\ 9 \\ \hline \end{array}$

13) $\begin{array}{r} 9 \\ \times\ 1 \\ \hline \end{array}$

14) $\begin{array}{r} 2 \\ \times\ 9 \\ \hline \end{array}$

15) $\begin{array}{r} 9 \\ \times\ 7 \\ \hline \end{array}$

16) $\begin{array}{r} 2 \\ \times\ 9 \\ \hline \end{array}$

17) $\begin{array}{r} 9 \\ \times\ 7 \\ \hline \end{array}$

18) $\begin{array}{r} 0 \\ \times\ 9 \\ \hline \end{array}$

19) $\begin{array}{r} 9 \\ \times\ 7 \\ \hline \end{array}$

20) $\begin{array}{r} 9 \\ \times\ 9 \\ \hline \end{array}$

21) $\begin{array}{r} 9 \\ \times\ 9 \\ \hline \end{array}$

22) $\begin{array}{r} 5 \\ \times\ 9 \\ \hline \end{array}$

23) $\begin{array}{r} 9 \\ \times\ 0 \\ \hline \end{array}$

24) $\begin{array}{r} 7 \\ \times\ 9 \\ \hline \end{array}$

25) $\begin{array}{r} 9 \\ \times\ 1 \\ \hline \end{array}$

26) $\begin{array}{r} 2 \\ \times\ 9 \\ \hline \end{array}$

27) $\begin{array}{r} 9 \\ \times\ 5 \\ \hline \end{array}$

28) $\begin{array}{r} 5 \\ \times\ 9 \\ \hline \end{array}$

29) $\begin{array}{r} 9 \\ \times\ 8 \\ \hline \end{array}$

30) $\begin{array}{r} 5 \\ \times\ 9 \\ \hline \end{array}$

31) $\begin{array}{r} 9 \\ \times\ 5 \\ \hline \end{array}$

32) $\begin{array}{r} 3 \\ \times\ 9 \\ \hline \end{array}$

33) $\begin{array}{r} 9 \\ \times\ 4 \\ \hline \end{array}$

34) $\begin{array}{r} 9 \\ \times\ 9 \\ \hline \end{array}$

35) $\begin{array}{r} 9 \\ \times\ 9 \\ \hline \end{array}$

36) $\begin{array}{r} 2 \\ \times\ 9 \\ \hline \end{array}$

37) $\begin{array}{r} 9 \\ \times\ 3 \\ \hline \end{array}$

38) $\begin{array}{r} 8 \\ \times\ 9 \\ \hline \end{array}$

39) $\begin{array}{r} 9 \\ \times\ 8 \\ \hline \end{array}$

40) $\begin{array}{r} 5 \\ \times\ 9 \\ \hline \end{array}$

41) $\begin{array}{r} 9 \\ \times\ 7 \\ \hline \end{array}$

42) $\begin{array}{r} 0 \\ \times\ 9 \\ \hline \end{array}$

43) $\begin{array}{r} 9 \\ \times\ 4 \\ \hline \end{array}$

44) $\begin{array}{r} 1 \\ \times\ 9 \\ \hline \end{array}$

45) $\begin{array}{r} 9 \\ \times\ 1 \\ \hline \end{array}$

46) $\begin{array}{r} 2 \\ \times\ 9 \\ \hline \end{array}$

47) $\begin{array}{r} 9 \\ \times\ 3 \\ \hline \end{array}$

48) $\begin{array}{r} 4 \\ \times\ 9 \\ \hline \end{array}$

49) $\begin{array}{r} 9 \\ \times\ 8 \\ \hline \end{array}$

50) $\begin{array}{r} 7 \\ \times\ 9 \\ \hline \end{array}$

51) $\begin{array}{r} 9 \\ \times\ 6 \\ \hline \end{array}$

52) $\begin{array}{r} 3 \\ \times\ 9 \\ \hline \end{array}$

53) $\begin{array}{r} 9 \\ \times\ 7 \\ \hline \end{array}$

54) $\begin{array}{r} 3 \\ \times\ 9 \\ \hline \end{array}$

55) $\begin{array}{r} 9 \\ \times\ 6 \\ \hline \end{array}$

56) $\begin{array}{r} 1 \\ \times\ 9 \\ \hline \end{array}$

57) $\begin{array}{r} 9 \\ \times\ 8 \\ \hline \end{array}$

58) $\begin{array}{r} 3 \\ \times\ 9 \\ \hline \end{array}$

59) $\begin{array}{r} 9 \\ \times\ 8 \\ \hline \end{array}$

60) $\begin{array}{r} 2 \\ \times\ 9 \\ \hline \end{array}$

1) 9
   × 5

2) 9
   × 9

3) 9
   × 9

4) 8
   × 9

5) 9
   × 3

6) 0
   × 9

7) 9
   × 2

8) 6
   × 9

9) 9
   × 9

10) 3
    × 9

11) 9
    × 8

12) 3
    × 9

13) 9
    × 8

14) 1
    × 9

15) 9
    × 3

16) 1
    × 9

17) 9
    × 9

18) 1
    × 9

19) 9
    × 0

20) 3
    × 9

21) 9
    × 0

22) 7
    × 9

23) 9
    × 8

24) 2
    × 9

25) 9
    × 6

26) 5
    × 9

27) 9
    × 4

28) 4
    × 9

29) 9
    × 5

30) 8
    × 9

31) 9
    × 4

32) 7
    × 9

33) 9
    × 6

34) 1
    × 9

35) 9
    × 4

36) 4
    × 9

37) 9
    × 7

38) 1
    × 9

39) 9
    × 6

40) 8
    × 9

41) 9
    × 6

42) 5
    × 9

43) 9
    × 4

44) 0
    × 9

45) 9
    × 5

46) 4
    × 9

47) 9
    × 3

48) 4
    × 9

49) 9
    × 9

50) 6
    × 9

51) 9
    × 3

52) 6
    × 9

53) 9
    × 7

54) 8
    × 9

55) 9
    × 9

56) 5
    × 9

57) 9
    × 0

58) 8
    × 9

59) 9
    × 2

60) 0
    × 9

Name: _____

Let's Multiply 9

Day /100

Date: _____
Time: _____

Score /60

1) $\begin{array}{r} 9 \\ \times\ 8 \\ \hline \end{array}$
2) $\begin{array}{r} 7 \\ \times\ 9 \\ \hline \end{array}$
3) $\begin{array}{r} 9 \\ \times\ 4 \\ \hline \end{array}$
4) $\begin{array}{r} 9 \\ \times\ 9 \\ \hline \end{array}$
5) $\begin{array}{r} 9 \\ \times\ 5 \\ \hline \end{array}$
6) $\begin{array}{r} 4 \\ \times\ 9 \\ \hline \end{array}$

7) $\begin{array}{r} 9 \\ \times\ 7 \\ \hline \end{array}$
8) $\begin{array}{r} 7 \\ \times\ 9 \\ \hline \end{array}$
9) $\begin{array}{r} 9 \\ \times\ 5 \\ \hline \end{array}$
10) $\begin{array}{r} 0 \\ \times\ 9 \\ \hline \end{array}$
11) $\begin{array}{r} 9 \\ \times\ 7 \\ \hline \end{array}$
12) $\begin{array}{r} 3 \\ \times\ 9 \\ \hline \end{array}$

13) $\begin{array}{r} 9 \\ \times\ 3 \\ \hline \end{array}$
14) $\begin{array}{r} 9 \\ \times\ 9 \\ \hline \end{array}$
15) $\begin{array}{r} 9 \\ \times\ 9 \\ \hline \end{array}$
16) $\begin{array}{r} 1 \\ \times\ 9 \\ \hline \end{array}$
17) $\begin{array}{r} 9 \\ \times\ 7 \\ \hline \end{array}$
18) $\begin{array}{r} 4 \\ \times\ 9 \\ \hline \end{array}$

19) $\begin{array}{r} 9 \\ \times\ 8 \\ \hline \end{array}$
20) $\begin{array}{r} 6 \\ \times\ 9 \\ \hline \end{array}$
21) $\begin{array}{r} 9 \\ \times\ 3 \\ \hline \end{array}$
22) $\begin{array}{r} 7 \\ \times\ 9 \\ \hline \end{array}$
23) $\begin{array}{r} 9 \\ \times\ 6 \\ \hline \end{array}$
24) $\begin{array}{r} 9 \\ \times\ 9 \\ \hline \end{array}$

25) $\begin{array}{r} 9 \\ \times\ 5 \\ \hline \end{array}$
26) $\begin{array}{r} 5 \\ \times\ 9 \\ \hline \end{array}$
27) $\begin{array}{r} 9 \\ \times\ 2 \\ \hline \end{array}$
28) $\begin{array}{r} 5 \\ \times\ 9 \\ \hline \end{array}$
29) $\begin{array}{r} 9 \\ \times\ 8 \\ \hline \end{array}$
30) $\begin{array}{r} 8 \\ \times\ 9 \\ \hline \end{array}$

31) $\begin{array}{r} 9 \\ \times\ 2 \\ \hline \end{array}$
32) $\begin{array}{r} 0 \\ \times\ 9 \\ \hline \end{array}$
33) $\begin{array}{r} 9 \\ \times\ 8 \\ \hline \end{array}$
34) $\begin{array}{r} 3 \\ \times\ 9 \\ \hline \end{array}$
35) $\begin{array}{r} 9 \\ \times\ 3 \\ \hline \end{array}$
36) $\begin{array}{r} 4 \\ \times\ 9 \\ \hline \end{array}$

37) $\begin{array}{r} 9 \\ \times\ 6 \\ \hline \end{array}$
38) $\begin{array}{r} 0 \\ \times\ 9 \\ \hline \end{array}$
39) $\begin{array}{r} 9 \\ \times\ 3 \\ \hline \end{array}$
40) $\begin{array}{r} 6 \\ \times\ 9 \\ \hline \end{array}$
41) $\begin{array}{r} 9 \\ \times\ 9 \\ \hline \end{array}$
42) $\begin{array}{r} 3 \\ \times\ 9 \\ \hline \end{array}$

43) $\begin{array}{r} 9 \\ \times\ 4 \\ \hline \end{array}$
44) $\begin{array}{r} 7 \\ \times\ 9 \\ \hline \end{array}$
45) $\begin{array}{r} 9 \\ \times\ 5 \\ \hline \end{array}$
46) $\begin{array}{r} 4 \\ \times\ 9 \\ \hline \end{array}$
47) $\begin{array}{r} 9 \\ \times\ 3 \\ \hline \end{array}$
48) $\begin{array}{r} 7 \\ \times\ 9 \\ \hline \end{array}$

49) $\begin{array}{r} 9 \\ \times\ 8 \\ \hline \end{array}$
50) $\begin{array}{r} 2 \\ \times\ 9 \\ \hline \end{array}$
51) $\begin{array}{r} 9 \\ \times\ 7 \\ \hline \end{array}$
52) $\begin{array}{r} 8 \\ \times\ 9 \\ \hline \end{array}$
53) $\begin{array}{r} 9 \\ \times\ 9 \\ \hline \end{array}$
54) $\begin{array}{r} 8 \\ \times\ 9 \\ \hline \end{array}$

55) $\begin{array}{r} 9 \\ \times\ 3 \\ \hline \end{array}$
56) $\begin{array}{r} 5 \\ \times\ 9 \\ \hline \end{array}$
57) $\begin{array}{r} 9 \\ \times\ 8 \\ \hline \end{array}$
58) $\begin{array}{r} 8 \\ \times\ 9 \\ \hline \end{array}$
59) $\begin{array}{r} 9 \\ \times\ 6 \\ \hline \end{array}$
60) $\begin{array}{r} 9 \\ \times\ 9 \\ \hline \end{array}$

Name: _____

Let's Multiply 10

Day
/100

Date: _____

Time: _____

Score
/60

1) 10
  × 6

2)   9
  × 10

3) 10
  × 6

4)   7
  × 10

5) 10
  × 7

6)   3
  × 10

7) 10
  × 8

8)   0
  × 10

9) 10
  × 1

10)   0
  × 10

11) 10
  × 0

12)   1
  × 10

13) 10
  × 1

14)   9
  × 10

15) 10
  × 7

16)   9
  × 10

17) 10
  × 4

18)   0
  × 10

19) 10
  × 0

20)   8
  × 10

21) 10
  × 3

22)   1
  × 10

23) 10
  × 7

24)   8
  × 10

25) 10
  × 7

26)   8
  × 10

27) 10
  × 0

28)   7
  × 10

29) 10
  × 0

30)   5
  × 10

31) 10
  × 6

32)   3
  × 10

33) 10
  × 0

34)   5
  × 10

35) 10
  × 4

36)   5
  × 10

37) 10
  × 4

38)   1
  × 10

39) 10
  × 5

40)   7
  × 10

41) 10
  × 8

42)   9
  × 10

43) 10
  × 3

44)   9
  × 10

45) 10
  × 9

46)   0
  × 10

47) 10
  × 4

48)   6
  × 10

49) 10
  × 6

50)   7
  × 10

51) 10
  × 7

52)   1
  × 10

53) 10
  × 3

54)   5
  × 10

55) 10
  × 6

56)   9
  × 10

57) 10
  × 0

58)   9
  × 10

59) 10
  × 3

60)   3
  × 10

1) 10
  × 9

2)   2
  × 10

3) 10
  × 0

4)   9
  × 10

5) 10
  × 4

6)   6
  × 10

7) 10
  × 6

8)   3
  × 10

9) 10
  × 8

10)   1
  × 10

11) 10
  × 5

12)   5
  × 10

13) 10
  × 6

14)   1
  × 10

15) 10
  × 6

16)   6
  × 10

17) 10
  × 0

18)   1
  × 10

19) 10
  × 9

20)   5
  × 10

21) 10
  × 8

22)   5
  × 10

23) 10
  × 7

24)   5
  × 10

25) 10
  × 5

26)   4
  × 10

27) 10
  × 5

28)   0
  × 10

29) 10
  × 5

30)   9
  × 10

31) 10
  × 2

32)   6
  × 10

33) 10
  × 0

34)   1
  × 10

35) 10
  × 4

36)   3
  × 10

37) 10
  × 7

38)   4
  × 10

39) 10
  × 2

40)   0
  × 10

41) 10
  × 2

42)   2
  × 10

43) 10
  × 2

44)   0
  × 10

45) 10
  × 3

46)   0
  × 10

47) 10
  × 3

48)   4
  × 10

49) 10
  × 5

50)   8
  × 10

51) 10
  × 6

52)   0
  × 10

53) 10
  × 0

54)   5
  × 10

55) 10
  × 6

56)   3
  × 10

57) 10
  × 8

58)   7
  × 10

59) 10
  × 6

60)   3
  × 10

1) 10
  × 9

2)   9
  × 10

3) 10
  × 0

4)   2
  × 10

5) 10
  × 4

6)   9
  × 10

7) 10
  × 2

8)   5
  × 10

9) 10
  × 0

10)   6
  × 10

11) 10
  × 4

12)   1
  × 10

13) 10
  × 7

14)   5
  × 10

15) 10
  × 5

16)   9
  × 10

17) 10
  × 4

18)   2
  × 10

19) 10
  × 3

20)   0
  × 10

21) 10
  × 3

22)   9
  × 10

23) 10
  × 3

24)   1
  × 10

25) 10
  × 4

26)   2
  × 10

27) 10
  × 2

28)   5
  × 10

29) 10
  × 1

30)   2
  × 10

31) 10
  × 2

32)   9
  × 10

33) 10
  × 9

34)   5
  × 10

35) 10
  × 0

36)   2
  × 10

37) 10
  × 1

38)   3
  × 10

39) 10
  × 6

40)   2
  × 10

41) 10
  × 8

42)   0
  × 10

43) 10
  × 7

44)   1
  × 10

45) 10
  × 6

46)   2
  × 10

47) 10
  × 3

48)   4
  × 10

49) 10
  × 6

50)   3
  × 10

51) 10
  × 0

52)   8
  × 10

53) 10
  × 2

54)   2
  × 10

55) 10
  × 1

56)   7
  × 10

57) 10
  × 6

58)   5
  × 10

59) 10
  × 1

60)   6
  × 10

Name: _____   Let's Multiply 10

Day
/100

Date: _____
Time: _____

Score
/60

1)   10
  × 2

2)   8
  × 10

3)   10
  × 1

4)   6
  × 10

5)   10
  × 5

6)   3
  × 10

7)   10
  × 5

8)   2
  × 10

9)   10
  × 6

10)   6
  × 10

11)   10
  × 6

12)   9
  × 10

13)   10
  × 5

14)   0
  × 10

15)   10
  × 9

16)   9
  × 10

17)   10
  × 3

18)   0
  × 10

19)   10
  × 9

20)   1
  × 10

21)   10
  × 5

22)   1
  × 10

23)   10
  × 7

24)   8
  × 10

25)   10
  × 3

26)   9
  × 10

27)   10
  × 7

28)   6
  × 10

29)   10
  × 6

30)   0
  × 10

31)   10
  × 6

32)   4
  × 10

33)   10
  × 7

34)   4
  × 10

35)   10
  × 7

36)   0
  × 10

37)   10
  × 3

38)   4
  × 10

39)   10
  × 6

40)   6
  × 10

41)   10
  × 3

42)   5
  × 10

43)   10
  × 8

44)   5
  × 10

45)   10
  × 8

46)   4
  × 10

47)   10
  × 8

48)   6
  × 10

49)   10
  × 0

50)   4
  × 10

51)   10
  × 9

52)   4
  × 10

53)   10
  × 8

54)   7
  × 10

55)   10
  × 4

56)   0
  × 10

57)   10
  × 0

58)   2
  × 10

59)   10
  × 5

60)   4
  × 10

Let's Multiply 10

1)
```
   10
×   9
```

2)
```
    7
× 10
```

3)
```
   10
×   8
```

4)
```
    8
× 10
```

5)
```
   10
×   3
```

6)
```
    8
× 10
```

7)
```
   10
×   6
```

8)
```
    0
× 10
```

9)
```
   10
×   6
```

10)
```
    1
× 10
```

11)
```
   10
×   2
```

12)
```
    0
× 10
```

13)
```
   10
×   6
```

14)
```
    1
× 10
```

15)
```
   10
×   6
```

16)
```
    7
× 10
```

17)
```
   10
×   1
```

18)
```
    5
× 10
```

19)
```
   10
×   7
```

20)
```
    0
× 10
```

21)
```
   10
×   1
```

22)
```
    4
× 10
```

23)
```
   10
×   3
```

24)
```
    5
× 10
```

25)
```
   10
×   1
```

26)
```
    8
× 10
```

27)
```
   10
×   0
```

28)
```
    5
× 10
```

29)
```
   10
×   6
```

30)
```
    3
× 10
```

31)
```
   10
×   2
```

32)
```
    5
× 10
```

33)
```
   10
×   9
```

34)
```
    9
× 10
```

35)
```
   10
×   8
```

36)
```
    7
× 10
```

37)
```
   10
×   1
```

38)
```
    5
× 10
```

39)
```
   10
×   6
```

40)
```
    9
× 10
```

41)
```
   10
×   7
```

42)
```
    3
× 10
```

43)
```
   10
×   3
```

44)
```
    5
× 10
```

45)
```
   10
×   8
```

46)
```
    0
× 10
```

47)
```
   10
×   6
```

48)
```
    6
× 10
```

49)
```
   10
×   6
```

50)
```
    2
× 10
```

51)
```
   10
×   1
```

52)
```
    2
× 10
```

53)
```
   10
×   9
```

54)
```
    8
× 10
```

55)
```
   10
×   2
```

56)
```
    5
× 10
```

57)
```
   10
×   9
```

58)
```
    7
× 10
```

59)
```
   10
×   3
```

60)
```
    2
× 10
```

Name: _____

Let's Multiply 10

Day
/100

Date: _____

Time: _____

Score
/60

1)
```
   10
×   8
```

2)
```
    0
× 10
```

3)
```
   10
×   8
```

4)
```
    2
× 10
```

5)
```
   10
×   9
```

6)
```
    4
× 10
```

7)
```
   10
×   4
```

8)
```
    8
× 10
```

9)
```
   10
×   2
```

10)
```
    2
× 10
```

11)
```
   10
×   6
```

12)
```
    9
× 10
```

13)
```
   10
×   1
```

14)
```
    6
× 10
```

15)
```
   10
×   2
```

16)
```
    1
× 10
```

17)
```
   10
×   6
```

18)
```
    7
× 10
```

19)
```
   10
×   8
```

20)
```
    0
× 10
```

21)
```
   10
×   3
```

22)
```
    3
× 10
```

23)
```
   10
×   3
```

24)
```
    8
× 10
```

25)
```
   10
×   9
```

26)
```
    3
× 10
```

27)
```
   10
×   6
```

28)
```
    6
× 10
```

29)
```
   10
×   9
```

30)
```
    8
× 10
```

31)
```
   10
×   0
```

32)
```
    3
× 10
```

33)
```
   10
×   2
```

34)
```
    1
× 10
```

35)
```
   10
×   8
```

36)
```
    8
× 10
```

37)
```
   10
×   1
```

38)
```
    9
× 10
```

39)
```
   10
×   6
```

40)
```
    3
× 10
```

41)
```
   10
×   9
```

42)
```
    6
× 10
```

43)
```
   10
×   6
```

44)
```
    1
× 10
```

45)
```
   10
×   2
```

46)
```
    3
× 10
```

47)
```
   10
×   9
```

48)
```
    1
× 10
```

49)
```
   10
×   9
```

50)
```
    0
× 10
```

51)
```
   10
×   7
```

52)
```
    0
× 10
```

53)
```
   10
×   5
```

54)
```
    7
× 10
```

55)
```
   10
×   1
```

56)
```
    1
× 10
```

57)
```
   10
×   2
```

58)
```
    8
× 10
```

59)
```
   10
×   8
```

60)
```
    1
× 10
```

Name: _____

Let's Multiply 10

Day /100

Date: _____

Time: _____

Score /60

1) 10 × 4

2) 9 × 10

3) 10 × 6

4) 6 × 10

5) 10 × 1

6) 6 × 10

7) 10 × 9

8) 8 × 10

9) 10 × 9

10) 1 × 10

11) 10 × 6

12) 3 × 10

13) 10 × 8

14) 3 × 10

15) 10 × 4

16) 9 × 10

17) 10 × 6

18) 0 × 10

19) 10 × 5

20) 5 × 10

21) 10 × 3

22) 0 × 10

23) 10 × 6

24) 8 × 10

25) 10 × 7

26) 6 × 10

27) 10 × 5

28) 6 × 10

29) 10 × 4

30) 5 × 10

31) 10 × 9

32) 2 × 10

33) 10 × 6

34) 2 × 10

35) 10 × 5

36) 5 × 10

37) 10 × 3

38) 9 × 10

39) 10 × 8

40) 6 × 10

41) 10 × 8

42) 4 × 10

43) 10 × 2

44) 0 × 10

45) 10 × 2

46) 8 × 10

47) 10 × 3

48) 6 × 10

49) 10 × 3

50) 3 × 10

51) 10 × 6

52) 3 × 10

53) 10 × 2

54) 8 × 10

55) 10 × 0

56) 9 × 10

57) 10 × 7

58) 0 × 10

59) 10 × 0

60) 9 × 10

Name: _____

Let's Multiply 11

Day
/100

Date: _____
Time: _____

Score
/60

1)　11
× 9

2)　　3
× 11

3)　11
× 1

4)　　3
× 11

5)　11
× 7

6)　　1
× 11

7)　11
× 7

8)　　1
× 11

9)　11
× 3

10)　　7
× 11

11)　11
× 2

12)　　5
× 11

13)　11
× 7

14)　　5
× 11

15)　11
× 3

16)　　0
× 11

17)　11
× 4

18)　　5
× 11

19)　11
× 9

20)　　4
× 11

21)　11
× 4

22)　　0
× 11

23)　11
× 3

24)　　0
× 11

25)　11
× 0

26)　　7
× 11

27)　11
× 1

28)　　0
× 11

29)　11
× 2

30)　　0
× 11

31)　11
× 5

32)　　5
× 11

33)　11
× 7

34)　　0
× 11

35)　11
× 2

36)　　5
× 11

37)　11
× 1

38)　　3
× 11

39)　11
× 0

40)　　6
× 11

41)　11
× 4

42)　　3
× 11

43)　11
× 9

44)　　2
× 11

45)　11
× 2

46)　　1
× 11

47)　11
× 0

48)　　8
× 11

49)　11
× 7

50)　　5
× 11

51)　11
× 1

52)　　1
× 11

53)　11
× 4

54)　　7
× 11

55)　11
× 1

56)　　7
× 11

57)　11
× 2

58)　　6
× 11

59)　11
× 9

60)　　8
× 11

1)
$$\begin{array}{r} 11 \\ \times\ 7 \\ \hline \end{array}$$

2)
$$\begin{array}{r} 6 \\ \times\ 11 \\ \hline \end{array}$$

3)
$$\begin{array}{r} 11 \\ \times\ 7 \\ \hline \end{array}$$

4)
$$\begin{array}{r} 4 \\ \times\ 11 \\ \hline \end{array}$$

5)
$$\begin{array}{r} 11 \\ \times\ 8 \\ \hline \end{array}$$

6)
$$\begin{array}{r} 9 \\ \times\ 11 \\ \hline \end{array}$$

7)
$$\begin{array}{r} 11 \\ \times\ 7 \\ \hline \end{array}$$

8)
$$\begin{array}{r} 8 \\ \times\ 11 \\ \hline \end{array}$$

9)
$$\begin{array}{r} 11 \\ \times\ 2 \\ \hline \end{array}$$

10)
$$\begin{array}{r} 0 \\ \times\ 11 \\ \hline \end{array}$$

11)
$$\begin{array}{r} 11 \\ \times\ 3 \\ \hline \end{array}$$

12)
$$\begin{array}{r} 6 \\ \times\ 11 \\ \hline \end{array}$$

13)
$$\begin{array}{r} 11 \\ \times\ 2 \\ \hline \end{array}$$

14)
$$\begin{array}{r} 7 \\ \times\ 11 \\ \hline \end{array}$$

15)
$$\begin{array}{r} 11 \\ \times\ 4 \\ \hline \end{array}$$

16)
$$\begin{array}{r} 0 \\ \times\ 11 \\ \hline \end{array}$$

17)
$$\begin{array}{r} 11 \\ \times\ 9 \\ \hline \end{array}$$

18)
$$\begin{array}{r} 4 \\ \times\ 11 \\ \hline \end{array}$$

19)
$$\begin{array}{r} 11 \\ \times\ 9 \\ \hline \end{array}$$

20)
$$\begin{array}{r} 2 \\ \times\ 11 \\ \hline \end{array}$$

21)
$$\begin{array}{r} 11 \\ \times\ 5 \\ \hline \end{array}$$

22)
$$\begin{array}{r} 7 \\ \times\ 11 \\ \hline \end{array}$$

23)
$$\begin{array}{r} 11 \\ \times\ 0 \\ \hline \end{array}$$

24)
$$\begin{array}{r} 6 \\ \times\ 11 \\ \hline \end{array}$$

25)
$$\begin{array}{r} 11 \\ \times\ 0 \\ \hline \end{array}$$

26)
$$\begin{array}{r} 9 \\ \times\ 11 \\ \hline \end{array}$$

27)
$$\begin{array}{r} 11 \\ \times\ 0 \\ \hline \end{array}$$

28)
$$\begin{array}{r} 8 \\ \times\ 11 \\ \hline \end{array}$$

29)
$$\begin{array}{r} 11 \\ \times\ 9 \\ \hline \end{array}$$

30)
$$\begin{array}{r} 3 \\ \times\ 11 \\ \hline \end{array}$$

31)
$$\begin{array}{r} 11 \\ \times\ 0 \\ \hline \end{array}$$

32)
$$\begin{array}{r} 9 \\ \times\ 11 \\ \hline \end{array}$$

33)
$$\begin{array}{r} 11 \\ \times\ 0 \\ \hline \end{array}$$

34)
$$\begin{array}{r} 6 \\ \times\ 11 \\ \hline \end{array}$$

35)
$$\begin{array}{r} 11 \\ \times\ 9 \\ \hline \end{array}$$

36)
$$\begin{array}{r} 2 \\ \times\ 11 \\ \hline \end{array}$$

37)
$$\begin{array}{r} 11 \\ \times\ 7 \\ \hline \end{array}$$

38)
$$\begin{array}{r} 5 \\ \times\ 11 \\ \hline \end{array}$$

39)
$$\begin{array}{r} 11 \\ \times\ 0 \\ \hline \end{array}$$

40)
$$\begin{array}{r} 4 \\ \times\ 11 \\ \hline \end{array}$$

41)
$$\begin{array}{r} 11 \\ \times\ 5 \\ \hline \end{array}$$

42)
$$\begin{array}{r} 2 \\ \times\ 11 \\ \hline \end{array}$$

43)
$$\begin{array}{r} 11 \\ \times\ 8 \\ \hline \end{array}$$

44)
$$\begin{array}{r} 7 \\ \times\ 11 \\ \hline \end{array}$$

45)
$$\begin{array}{r} 11 \\ \times\ 7 \\ \hline \end{array}$$

46)
$$\begin{array}{r} 6 \\ \times\ 11 \\ \hline \end{array}$$

47)
$$\begin{array}{r} 11 \\ \times\ 5 \\ \hline \end{array}$$

48)
$$\begin{array}{r} 4 \\ \times\ 11 \\ \hline \end{array}$$

49)
$$\begin{array}{r} 11 \\ \times\ 6 \\ \hline \end{array}$$

50)
$$\begin{array}{r} 7 \\ \times\ 11 \\ \hline \end{array}$$

51)
$$\begin{array}{r} 11 \\ \times\ 7 \\ \hline \end{array}$$

52)
$$\begin{array}{r} 7 \\ \times\ 11 \\ \hline \end{array}$$

53)
$$\begin{array}{r} 11 \\ \times\ 8 \\ \hline \end{array}$$

54)
$$\begin{array}{r} 4 \\ \times\ 11 \\ \hline \end{array}$$

55)
$$\begin{array}{r} 11 \\ \times\ 4 \\ \hline \end{array}$$

56)
$$\begin{array}{r} 1 \\ \times\ 11 \\ \hline \end{array}$$

57)
$$\begin{array}{r} 11 \\ \times\ 1 \\ \hline \end{array}$$

58)
$$\begin{array}{r} 0 \\ \times\ 11 \\ \hline \end{array}$$

59)
$$\begin{array}{r} 11 \\ \times\ 6 \\ \hline \end{array}$$

60)
$$\begin{array}{r} 6 \\ \times\ 11 \\ \hline \end{array}$$

Name: _____

Let's Multiply 11

Day
/100

Date: _____
Time: _____

Score
/60

1) 11
  × 0

2)   9
  × 11

3) 11
  × 7

4)   7
  × 11

5) 11
  × 2

6)   2
  × 11

7) 11
  × 1

8)   0
  × 11

9) 11
  × 5

10)   6
  × 11

11) 11
  × 9

12)   8
  × 11

13) 11
  × 1

14)   5
  × 11

15) 11
  × 3

16)   6
  × 11

17) 11
  × 7

18)   5
  × 11

19) 11
  × 9

20)   3
  × 11

21) 11
  × 2

22)   9
  × 11

23) 11
  × 4

24)   3
  × 11

25) 11
  × 5

26)   3
  × 11

27) 11
  × 8

28)   6
  × 11

29) 11
  × 5

30)   4
  × 11

31) 11
  × 3

32)   8
  × 11

33) 11
  × 6

34)   5
  × 11

35) 11
  × 0

36)   8
  × 11

37) 11
  × 4

38)   0
  × 11

39) 11
  × 3

40)   3
  × 11

41) 11
  × 2

42)   1
  × 11

43) 11
  × 3

44)   2
  × 11

45) 11
  × 0

46)   1
  × 11

47) 11
  × 1

48)   2
  × 11

49) 11
  × 1

50)   4
  × 11

51) 11
  × 5

52)   2
  × 11

53) 11
  × 9

54)   5
  × 11

55) 11
  × 8

56)   1
  × 11

57) 11
  × 0

58)   0
  × 11

59) 11
  × 9

60)   7
  × 11

Name: _____

Let's Multiply 11

Day /100

Date: _____

Time: _____

Score /60

1) 11
× 3

2) 7
× 11

3) 11
× 5

4) 6
× 11

5) 11
× 5

6) 1
× 11

7) 11
× 5

8) 2
× 11

9) 11
× 0

10) 5
× 11

11) 11
× 8

12) 7
× 11

13) 11
× 4

14) 6
× 11

15) 11
× 2

16) 3
× 11

17) 11
× 8

18) 0
× 11

19) 11
× 3

20) 7
× 11

21) 11
× 4

22) 3
× 11

23) 11
× 4

24) 1
× 11

25) 11
× 3

26) 6
× 11

27) 11
× 2

28) 4
× 11

29) 11
× 5

30) 9
× 11

31) 11
× 1

32) 6
× 11

33) 11
× 7

34) 4
× 11

35) 11
× 5

36) 5
× 11

37) 11
× 4

38) 1
× 11

39) 11
× 7

40) 1
× 11

41) 11
× 1

42) 6
× 11

43) 11
× 3

44) 9
× 11

45) 11
× 1

46) 9
× 11

47) 11
× 6

48) 8
× 11

49) 11
× 2

50) 0
× 11

51) 11
× 6

52) 0
× 11

53) 11
× 2

54) 4
× 11

55) 11
× 5

56) 3
× 11

57) 11
× 5

58) 0
× 11

59) 11
× 3

60) 6
× 11

1)   11 × 3

2)   3 × 11

3)   11 × 4

4)   4 × 11

5)   11 × 6

6)   4 × 11

7)   11 × 7

8)   0 × 11

9)   11 × 5

10)   5 × 11

11)   11 × 4

12)   3 × 11

13)   11 × 1

14)   4 × 11

15)   11 × 7

16)   5 × 11

17)   11 × 8

18)   1 × 11

19)   11 × 1

20)   1 × 11

21)   11 × 4

22)   8 × 11

23)   11 × 4

24)   1 × 11

25)   11 × 6

26)   8 × 11

27)   11 × 5

28)   1 × 11

29)   11 × 4

30)   2 × 11

31)   11 × 7

32)   1 × 11

33)   11 × 4

34)   7 × 11

35)   11 × 9

36)   7 × 11

37)   11 × 0

38)   2 × 11

39)   11 × 9

40)   7 × 11

41)   11 × 8

42)   7 × 11

43)   11 × 2

44)   0 × 11

45)   11 × 0

46)   3 × 11

47)   11 × 3

48)   0 × 11

49)   11 × 2

50)   5 × 11

51)   11 × 5

52)   3 × 11

53)   11 × 6

54)   0 × 11

55)   11 × 8

56)   2 × 11

57)   11 × 5

58)   9 × 11

59)   11 × 9

60)   0 × 11

Name: _____

Let's Multiply 11

Day /100

Date: _____

Time: _____

Score /60

1) 11
  × 2

2)   7
  × 11

3) 11
  × 6

4)   0
  × 11

5) 11
  × 7

6)   9
  × 11

7) 11
  × 5

8)   6
  × 11

9) 11
  × 7

10)   1
  × 11

11) 11
  × 6

12)   7
  × 11

13) 11
  × 4

14)   1
  × 11

15) 11
  × 3

16)   9
  × 11

17) 11
  × 9

18)   4
  × 11

19) 11
  × 4

20)   7
  × 11

21) 11
  × 5

22)   9
  × 11

23) 11
  × 2

24)   4
  × 11

25) 11
  × 3

26)   3
  × 11

27) 11
  × 8

28)   5
  × 11

29) 11
  × 8

30)   8
  × 11

31) 11
  × 7

32)   0
  × 11

33) 11
  × 4

34)   2
  × 11

35) 11
  × 0

36)   1
  × 11

37) 11
  × 2

38)   2
  × 11

39) 11
  × 2

40)   9
  × 11

41) 11
  × 9

42)   5
  × 11

43) 11
  × 6

44)   8
  × 11

45) 11
  × 1

46)   8
  × 11

47) 11
  × 4

48)   8
  × 11

49) 11
  × 7

50)   8
  × 11

51) 11
  × 3

52)   2
  × 11

53) 11
  × 5

54)   8
  × 11

55) 11
  × 5

56)   6
  × 11

57) 11
  × 5

58)   5
  × 11

59) 11
  × 4

60)   4
  × 11

1) 11 × 5

2) 8 × 11

3) 11 × 8

4) 3 × 11

5) 11 × 2

6) 5 × 11

7) 11 × 0

8) 5 × 11

9) 11 × 2

10) 1 × 11

11) 11 × 1

12) 5 × 11

13) 11 × 6

14) 5 × 11

15) 11 × 6

16) 7 × 11

17) 11 × 5

18) 2 × 11

19) 11 × 9

20) 4 × 11

21) 11 × 4

22) 7 × 11

23) 11 × 6

24) 3 × 11

25) 11 × 0

26) 4 × 11

27) 11 × 6

28) 1 × 11

29) 11 × 9

30) 4 × 11

31) 11 × 4

32) 2 × 11

33) 11 × 9

34) 5 × 11

35) 11 × 5

36) 2 × 11

37) 11 × 5

38) 8 × 11

39) 11 × 9

40) 4 × 11

41) 11 × 5

42) 5 × 11

43) 11 × 4

44) 0 × 11

45) 11 × 4

46) 1 × 11

47) 11 × 9

48) 8 × 11

49) 11 × 9

50) 8 × 11

51) 11 × 3

52) 2 × 11

53) 11 × 7

54) 8 × 11

55) 11 × 5

56) 2 × 11

57) 11 × 2

58) 2 × 11

59) 11 × 8

60) 9 × 11

Name: _____

Let's Multiply 12

Day /100

Date: _____
Time: _____

Score /60

1) 12
  × 2

2)   7
  × 12

3) 12
  × 8

4)   7
  × 12

5) 12
  × 1

6)   6
  × 12

7) 12
  × 9

8)   0
  × 12

9) 12
  × 7

10) 7
  × 12

11) 12
  × 2

12) 5
  × 12

13) 12
  × 2

14) 9
  × 12

15) 12
  × 1

16) 6
  × 12

17) 12
  × 3

18) 2
  × 12

19) 12
  × 1

20) 9
  × 12

21) 12
  × 2

22) 4
  × 12

23) 12
  × 0

24) 9
  × 12

25) 12
  × 5

26) 8
  × 12

27) 12
  × 1

28) 0
  × 12

29) 12
  × 3

30) 9
  × 12

31) 12
  × 2

32) 8
  × 12

33) 12
  × 1

34) 4
  × 12

35) 12
  × 1

36) 7
  × 12

37) 12
  × 2

38) 2
  × 12

39) 12
  × 8

40) 1
  × 12

41) 12
  × 6

42) 9
  × 12

43) 12
  × 3

44) 4
  × 12

45) 12
  × 9

46) 2
  × 12

47) 12
  × 1

48) 6
  × 12

49) 12
  × 0

50) 6
  × 12

51) 12
  × 3

52) 7
  × 12

53) 12
  × 6

54) 4
  × 12

55) 12
  × 1

56) 1
  × 12

57) 12
  × 8

58) 1
  × 12

59) 12
  × 1

60) 8
  × 12

1) 12 × 9

2) 1 × 12

3) 12 × 8

4) 5 × 12

5) 12 × 5

6) 8 × 12

7) 12 × 5

8) 4 × 12

9) 12 × 4

10) 6 × 12

11) 12 × 9

12) 3 × 12

13) 12 × 2

14) 5 × 12

15) 12 × 8

16) 4 × 12

17) 12 × 3

18) 1 × 12

19) 12 × 0

20) 5 × 12

21) 12 × 8

22) 5 × 12

23) 12 × 7

24) 6 × 12

25) 12 × 5

26) 2 × 12

27) 12 × 9

28) 5 × 12

29) 12 × 3

30) 8 × 12

31) 12 × 9

32) 4 × 12

33) 12 × 2

34) 5 × 12

35) 12 × 3

36) 0 × 12

37) 12 × 6

38) 7 × 12

39) 12 × 4

40) 8 × 12

41) 12 × 9

42) 0 × 12

43) 12 × 4

44) 8 × 12

45) 12 × 6

46) 6 × 12

47) 12 × 7

48) 0 × 12

49) 12 × 0

50) 7 × 12

51) 12 × 8

52) 9 × 12

53) 12 × 3

54) 4 × 12

55) 12 × 9

56) 9 × 12

57) 12 × 6

58) 8 × 12

59) 12 × 9

60) 3 × 12

Name: _____

Let's Multiply 12

Day
/100

Date: _____
Time: _____

Score
/60

1)   12
 × 9

2)   3
 × 12

3)   12
 × 5

4)   2
 × 12

5)   12
 × 5

6)   7
 × 12

7)   12
 × 3

8)   6
 × 12

9)   12
 × 2

10)   4
 × 12

11) 12
 × 5

12)   7
 × 12

13) 12
 × 3

14)   2
 × 12

15) 12
 × 0

16)   7
 × 12

17) 12
 × 3

18)   3
 × 12

19) 12
 × 4

20)   4
 × 12

21) 12
 × 8

22)   8
 × 12

23) 12
 × 2

24)   7
 × 12

25) 12
 × 8

26)   8
 × 12

27) 12
 × 2

28)   7
 × 12

29) 12
 × 7

30)   0
 × 12

31) 12
 × 7

32)   1
 × 12

33) 12
 × 8

34)   2
 × 12

35) 12
 × 3

36)   8
 × 12

37) 12
 × 2

38)   5
 × 12

39) 12
 × 0

40)   4
 × 12

41) 12
 × 0

42)   9
 × 12

43) 12
 × 3

44)   0
 × 12

45) 12
 × 8

46)   7
 × 12

47) 12
 × 8

48)   2
 × 12

49) 12
 × 7

50)   2
 × 12

51) 12
 × 2

52)   5
 × 12

53) 12
 × 8

54)   5
 × 12

55) 12
 × 5

56)   8
 × 12

57) 12
 × 2

58)   4
 × 12

59) 12
 × 0

60)   1
 × 12

Name: _____

Let's Multiply 12

Day /100

Date: _____

Time: _____

Score /60

1)   12
 × 7

2)   2
 × 12

3)   12
 × 5

4)   7
 × 12

5)   12
 × 6

6)   2
 × 12

7)   12
 × 0

8)   7
 × 12

9)   12
 × 1

10)   7
 × 12

11)   12
 × 9

12)   0
 × 12

13)   12
 × 4

14)   9
 × 12

15)   12
 × 2

16)   4
 × 12

17)   12
 × 3

18)   3
 × 12

19)   12
 × 4

20)   0
 × 12

21)   12
 × 3

22)   4
 × 12

23)   12
 × 1

24)   0
 × 12

25)   12
 × 4

26)   6
 × 12

27)   12
 × 0

28)   0
 × 12

29)   12
 × 1

30)   9
 × 12

31)   12
 × 6

32)   5
 × 12

33)   12
 × 1

34)   3
 × 12

35)   12
 × 9

36)   7
 × 12

37)   12
 × 1

38)   2
 × 12

39)   12
 × 6

40)   8
 × 12

41)   12
 × 5

42)   4
 × 12

43)   12
 × 7

44)   7
 × 12

45)   12
 × 4

46)   8
 × 12

47)   12
 × 3

48)   1
 × 12

49)   12
 × 4

50)   2
 × 12

51)   12
 × 9

52)   5
 × 12

53)   12
 × 9

54)   4
 × 12

55)   12
 × 4

56)   7
 × 12

57)   12
 × 1

58)   1
 × 12

59)   12
 × 6

60)   0
 × 12

Name: _____

Let's Multiply 12

Day /100

Date: _____
Time: _____

Score /60

1) 12
    × 4

2)   0
    × 12

3) 12
    × 8

4)   8
    × 12

5) 12
    × 4

6)   4
    × 12

7) 12
    × 3

8)   6
    × 12

9) 12
    × 2

10) 8
    × 12

11) 12
    × 3

12) 3
    × 12

13) 12
    × 8

14) 6
    × 12

15) 12
    × 8

16) 3
    × 12

17) 12
    × 9

18) 4
    × 12

19) 12
    × 7

20) 1
    × 12

21) 12
    × 3

22) 6
    × 12

23) 12
    × 1

24) 6
    × 12

25) 12
    × 1

26) 5
    × 12

27) 12
    × 3

28) 4
    × 12

29) 12
    × 3

30) 5
    × 12

31) 12
    × 4

32) 9
    × 12

33) 12
    × 8

34) 7
    × 12

35) 12
    × 3

36) 4
    × 12

37) 12
    × 5

38) 0
    × 12

39) 12
    × 8

40) 1
    × 12

41) 12
    × 9

42) 8
    × 12

43) 12
    × 3

44) 3
    × 12

45) 12
    × 7

46) 7
    × 12

47) 12
    × 2

48) 7
    × 12

49) 12
    × 6

50) 7
    × 12

51) 12
    × 3

52) 9
    × 12

53) 12
    × 3

54) 9
    × 12

55) 12
    × 0

56) 8
    × 12

57) 12
    × 1

58) 2
    × 12

59) 12
    × 7

60) 5
    × 12

Name: _____

Let's Multiply 12

Day /100

Date: _____

Time: _____

Score /60

1) 12 × 2

2) 8 × 12

3) 12 × 8

4) 6 × 12

5) 12 × 2

6) 8 × 12

7) 12 × 9

8) 5 × 12

9) 12 × 0

10) 2 × 12

11) 12 × 7

12) 9 × 12

13) 12 × 1

14) 0 × 12

15) 12 × 1

16) 4 × 12

17) 12 × 9

18) 1 × 12

19) 12 × 1

20) 7 × 12

21) 12 × 2

22) 0 × 12

23) 12 × 6

24) 0 × 12

25) 12 × 5

26) 0 × 12

27) 12 × 0

28) 7 × 12

29) 12 × 9

30) 3 × 12

31) 12 × 0

32) 3 × 12

33) 12 × 6

34) 9 × 12

35) 12 × 9

36) 8 × 12

37) 12 × 2

38) 8 × 12

39) 12 × 3

40) 8 × 12

41) 12 × 2

42) 8 × 12

43) 12 × 2

44) 2 × 12

45) 12 × 3

46) 6 × 12

47) 12 × 5

48) 7 × 12

49) 12 × 0

50) 6 × 12

51) 12 × 7

52) 6 × 12

53) 12 × 6

54) 0 × 12

55) 12 × 5

56) 2 × 12

57) 12 × 0

58) 6 × 12

59) 12 × 9

60) 4 × 12

Name: _____

Let's Multiply 12

Day
/100

Date: _____
Time: _____

Score
/60

1)
$$\begin{array}{r} 12 \\ \times\ 2 \\ \hline \end{array}$$

2)
$$\begin{array}{r} 6 \\ \times\ 12 \\ \hline \end{array}$$

3)
$$\begin{array}{r} 12 \\ \times\ 7 \\ \hline \end{array}$$

4)
$$\begin{array}{r} 4 \\ \times\ 12 \\ \hline \end{array}$$

5)
$$\begin{array}{r} 12 \\ \times\ 4 \\ \hline \end{array}$$

6)
$$\begin{array}{r} 7 \\ \times\ 12 \\ \hline \end{array}$$

7)
$$\begin{array}{r} 12 \\ \times\ 6 \\ \hline \end{array}$$

8)
$$\begin{array}{r} 3 \\ \times\ 12 \\ \hline \end{array}$$

9)
$$\begin{array}{r} 12 \\ \times\ 9 \\ \hline \end{array}$$

10)
$$\begin{array}{r} 6 \\ \times\ 12 \\ \hline \end{array}$$

11)
$$\begin{array}{r} 12 \\ \times\ 5 \\ \hline \end{array}$$

12)
$$\begin{array}{r} 7 \\ \times\ 12 \\ \hline \end{array}$$

13)
$$\begin{array}{r} 12 \\ \times\ 1 \\ \hline \end{array}$$

14)
$$\begin{array}{r} 0 \\ \times\ 12 \\ \hline \end{array}$$

15)
$$\begin{array}{r} 12 \\ \times\ 8 \\ \hline \end{array}$$

16)
$$\begin{array}{r} 3 \\ \times\ 12 \\ \hline \end{array}$$

17)
$$\begin{array}{r} 12 \\ \times\ 6 \\ \hline \end{array}$$

18)
$$\begin{array}{r} 9 \\ \times\ 12 \\ \hline \end{array}$$

19)
$$\begin{array}{r} 12 \\ \times\ 6 \\ \hline \end{array}$$

20)
$$\begin{array}{r} 6 \\ \times\ 12 \\ \hline \end{array}$$

21)
$$\begin{array}{r} 12 \\ \times\ 7 \\ \hline \end{array}$$

22)
$$\begin{array}{r} 9 \\ \times\ 12 \\ \hline \end{array}$$

23)
$$\begin{array}{r} 12 \\ \times\ 0 \\ \hline \end{array}$$

24)
$$\begin{array}{r} 0 \\ \times\ 12 \\ \hline \end{array}$$

25)
$$\begin{array}{r} 12 \\ \times\ 9 \\ \hline \end{array}$$

26)
$$\begin{array}{r} 7 \\ \times\ 12 \\ \hline \end{array}$$

27)
$$\begin{array}{r} 12 \\ \times\ 8 \\ \hline \end{array}$$

28)
$$\begin{array}{r} 7 \\ \times\ 12 \\ \hline \end{array}$$

29)
$$\begin{array}{r} 12 \\ \times\ 0 \\ \hline \end{array}$$

30)
$$\begin{array}{r} 2 \\ \times\ 12 \\ \hline \end{array}$$

31)
$$\begin{array}{r} 12 \\ \times\ 9 \\ \hline \end{array}$$

32)
$$\begin{array}{r} 8 \\ \times\ 12 \\ \hline \end{array}$$

33)
$$\begin{array}{r} 12 \\ \times\ 1 \\ \hline \end{array}$$

34)
$$\begin{array}{r} 8 \\ \times\ 12 \\ \hline \end{array}$$

35)
$$\begin{array}{r} 12 \\ \times\ 9 \\ \hline \end{array}$$

36)
$$\begin{array}{r} 7 \\ \times\ 12 \\ \hline \end{array}$$

37)
$$\begin{array}{r} 12 \\ \times\ 4 \\ \hline \end{array}$$

38)
$$\begin{array}{r} 4 \\ \times\ 12 \\ \hline \end{array}$$

39)
$$\begin{array}{r} 12 \\ \times\ 9 \\ \hline \end{array}$$

40)
$$\begin{array}{r} 3 \\ \times\ 12 \\ \hline \end{array}$$

41)
$$\begin{array}{r} 12 \\ \times\ 3 \\ \hline \end{array}$$

42)
$$\begin{array}{r} 6 \\ \times\ 12 \\ \hline \end{array}$$

43)
$$\begin{array}{r} 12 \\ \times\ 0 \\ \hline \end{array}$$

44)
$$\begin{array}{r} 1 \\ \times\ 12 \\ \hline \end{array}$$

45)
$$\begin{array}{r} 12 \\ \times\ 1 \\ \hline \end{array}$$

46)
$$\begin{array}{r} 6 \\ \times\ 12 \\ \hline \end{array}$$

47)
$$\begin{array}{r} 12 \\ \times\ 3 \\ \hline \end{array}$$

48)
$$\begin{array}{r} 7 \\ \times\ 12 \\ \hline \end{array}$$

49)
$$\begin{array}{r} 12 \\ \times\ 5 \\ \hline \end{array}$$

50)
$$\begin{array}{r} 4 \\ \times\ 12 \\ \hline \end{array}$$

51)
$$\begin{array}{r} 12 \\ \times\ 5 \\ \hline \end{array}$$

52)
$$\begin{array}{r} 2 \\ \times\ 12 \\ \hline \end{array}$$

53)
$$\begin{array}{r} 12 \\ \times\ 2 \\ \hline \end{array}$$

54)
$$\begin{array}{r} 7 \\ \times\ 12 \\ \hline \end{array}$$

55)
$$\begin{array}{r} 12 \\ \times\ 3 \\ \hline \end{array}$$

56)
$$\begin{array}{r} 2 \\ \times\ 12 \\ \hline \end{array}$$

57)
$$\begin{array}{r} 12 \\ \times\ 2 \\ \hline \end{array}$$

58)
$$\begin{array}{r} 6 \\ \times\ 12 \\ \hline \end{array}$$

59)
$$\begin{array}{r} 12 \\ \times\ 2 \\ \hline \end{array}$$

60)
$$\begin{array}{r} 6 \\ \times\ 12 \\ \hline \end{array}$$

Name: _____

Multiplying Numbers 0 to 12

Day /100

Date: _____
Time: _____

Score /60

1) 12 × 7

2) 8 × 5

3) 12 × 2

4) 4 × 4

5) 3 × 1

6) 3 × 5

7) 3 × 6

8) 7 × 9

9) 8 × 9

10) 0 × 0

11) 9 × 6

12) 1 × 1

13) 6 × 0

14) 7 × 1

15) 12 × 0

16) 8 × 12

17) 1 × 6

18) 8 × 0

19) 7 × 3

20) 7 × 8

21) 12 × 1

22) 5 × 5

23) 10 × 0

24) 10 × 11

25) 0 × 3

26) 6 × 1

27) 10 × 10

28) 1 × 10

29) 10 × 2

30) 1 × 12

31) 0 × 5

32) 1 × 8

33) 3 × 0

34) 2 × 3

35) 6 × 7

36) 3 × 6

37) 2 × 4

38) 10 × 11

39) 3 × 5

40) 3 × 3

41) 7 × 2

42) 7 × 6

43) 3 × 4

44) 5 × 2

45) 12 × 7

46) 6 × 6

47) 0 × 4

48) 0 × 0

49) 6 × 6

50) 4 × 2

51) 7 × 9

52) 9 × 9

53) 7 × 5

54) 8 × 12

55) 11 × 4

56) 5 × 11

57) 7 × 9

58) 3 × 5

59) 11 × 0

60) 10 × 12

Name: _____

Multiplying Numbers 0 to 12

Day /100

Date: _____
Time: _____

Score /60

1)   3
 × 5

2)   4
 × 11

3)   9
 × 8

4)   0
 × 6

5)   11
 × 0

6)   3
 × 12

7)   2
 × 1

8)   1
 × 8

9)   0
 × 0

10)   8
 × 12

11)   9
 × 1

12)   3
 × 2

13)   7
 × 4

14)   6
 × 8

15)   4
 × 8

16)   8
 × 5

17)   0
 × 7

18)   10
 × 0

19)   8
 × 10

20)   10
 × 8

21)   5
 × 5

22)   4
 × 6

23)   3
 × 8

24)   0
 × 0

25)   9
 × 7

26)   2
 × 8

27)   2
 × 2

28)   4
 × 10

29)   3
 × 4

30)   10
 × 3

31)   0
 × 5

32)   9
 × 10

33)   8
 × 3

34)   0
 × 2

35)   2
 × 5

36)   6
 × 6

37)   2
 × 1

38)   2
 × 6

39)   0
 × 7

40)   1
 × 8

41)   1
 × 6

42)   1
 × 6

43)   5
 × 10

44)   9
 × 12

45)   10
 × 10

46)   5
 × 12

47)   1
 × 9

48)   8
 × 0

49)   10
 × 9

50)   1
 × 3

51)   0
 × 7

52)   2
 × 10

53)   6
 × 7

54)   6
 × 9

55)   4
 × 2

56)   4
 × 3

57)   4
 × 1

58)   9
 × 5

59)   11
 × 0

60)   7
 × 7

Name: _____

Multiplying Numbers 0 to 12

Day /100

Date: _____

Time: _____

Score /60

1) 5×8

2) 10×2

3) 8×8

4) 3×4

5) 8×1

6) 4×1

7) 3×5

8) 5×4

9) 6×7

10) 10×5

11) 9×3

12) 4×7

13) 7×0

14) 6×10

15) 4×1

16) 0×4

17) 11×9

18) 9×11

19) 3×7

20) 2×6

21) 9×6

22) 10×6

23) 4×4

24) 9×2

25) 0×1

26) 10×2

27) 4×2

28) 5×12

29) 4×2

30) 8×6

31) 8×10

32) 6×7

33) 3×1

34) 6×10

35) 5×3

36) 5×8

37) 11×9

38) 2×11

39) 2×8

40) 2×5

41) 4×1

42) 1×11

43) 8×6

44) 4×1

45) 6×8

46) 3×4

47) 12×8

48) 0×5

49) 1×9

50) 0×5

51) 9×3

52) 5×3

53) 2×7

54) 7×7

55) 3×0

56) 8×11

57) 6×0

58) 1×10

59) 0×10

60) 3×8

Name: _____

Multiplying Numbers 0 to 12

Day /100

Date: _____
Time: _____

Score /60

1)
$\begin{array}{r} 0 \\ \times\ 8 \\ \hline \end{array}$

2)
$\begin{array}{r} 0 \\ \times\ 6 \\ \hline \end{array}$

3)
$\begin{array}{r} 12 \\ \times\ 4 \\ \hline \end{array}$

4)
$\begin{array}{r} 4 \\ \times\ 0 \\ \hline \end{array}$

5)
$\begin{array}{r} 5 \\ \times\ 2 \\ \hline \end{array}$

6)
$\begin{array}{r} 1 \\ \times\ 2 \\ \hline \end{array}$

7)
$\begin{array}{r} 7 \\ \times\ 2 \\ \hline \end{array}$

8)
$\begin{array}{r} 3 \\ \times\ 0 \\ \hline \end{array}$

9)
$\begin{array}{r} 5 \\ \times\ 9 \\ \hline \end{array}$

10)
$\begin{array}{r} 1 \\ \times\ 8 \\ \hline \end{array}$

11)
$\begin{array}{r} 10 \\ \times\ 6 \\ \hline \end{array}$

12)
$\begin{array}{r} 8 \\ \times\ 7 \\ \hline \end{array}$

13)
$\begin{array}{r} 10 \\ \times\ 5 \\ \hline \end{array}$

14)
$\begin{array}{r} 6 \\ \times\ 2 \\ \hline \end{array}$

15)
$\begin{array}{r} 8 \\ \times\ 3 \\ \hline \end{array}$

16)
$\begin{array}{r} 4 \\ \times\ 9 \\ \hline \end{array}$

17)
$\begin{array}{r} 7 \\ \times\ 8 \\ \hline \end{array}$

18)
$\begin{array}{r} 10 \\ \times\ 5 \\ \hline \end{array}$

19)
$\begin{array}{r} 11 \\ \times\ 10 \\ \hline \end{array}$

20)
$\begin{array}{r} 4 \\ \times\ 0 \\ \hline \end{array}$

21)
$\begin{array}{r} 12 \\ \times\ 1 \\ \hline \end{array}$

22)
$\begin{array}{r} 0 \\ \times\ 12 \\ \hline \end{array}$

23)
$\begin{array}{r} 7 \\ \times\ 7 \\ \hline \end{array}$

24)
$\begin{array}{r} 2 \\ \times\ 7 \\ \hline \end{array}$

25)
$\begin{array}{r} 5 \\ \times\ 1 \\ \hline \end{array}$

26)
$\begin{array}{r} 4 \\ \times\ 0 \\ \hline \end{array}$

27)
$\begin{array}{r} 11 \\ \times\ 10 \\ \hline \end{array}$

28)
$\begin{array}{r} 10 \\ \times\ 8 \\ \hline \end{array}$

29)
$\begin{array}{r} 5 \\ \times\ 10 \\ \hline \end{array}$

30)
$\begin{array}{r} 2 \\ \times\ 1 \\ \hline \end{array}$

31)
$\begin{array}{r} 5 \\ \times\ 5 \\ \hline \end{array}$

32)
$\begin{array}{r} 8 \\ \times\ 9 \\ \hline \end{array}$

33)
$\begin{array}{r} 4 \\ \times\ 0 \\ \hline \end{array}$

34)
$\begin{array}{r} 9 \\ \times\ 5 \\ \hline \end{array}$

35)
$\begin{array}{r} 5 \\ \times\ 5 \\ \hline \end{array}$

36)
$\begin{array}{r} 6 \\ \times\ 6 \\ \hline \end{array}$

37)
$\begin{array}{r} 5 \\ \times\ 1 \\ \hline \end{array}$

38)
$\begin{array}{r} 10 \\ \times\ 3 \\ \hline \end{array}$

39)
$\begin{array}{r} 9 \\ \times\ 3 \\ \hline \end{array}$

40)
$\begin{array}{r} 8 \\ \times\ 11 \\ \hline \end{array}$

41)
$\begin{array}{r} 9 \\ \times\ 9 \\ \hline \end{array}$

42)
$\begin{array}{r} 4 \\ \times\ 8 \\ \hline \end{array}$

43)
$\begin{array}{r} 10 \\ \times\ 4 \\ \hline \end{array}$

44)
$\begin{array}{r} 4 \\ \times\ 9 \\ \hline \end{array}$

45)
$\begin{array}{r} 1 \\ \times\ 10 \\ \hline \end{array}$

46)
$\begin{array}{r} 4 \\ \times\ 3 \\ \hline \end{array}$

47)
$\begin{array}{r} 3 \\ \times\ 5 \\ \hline \end{array}$

48)
$\begin{array}{r} 5 \\ \times\ 10 \\ \hline \end{array}$

49)
$\begin{array}{r} 11 \\ \times\ 8 \\ \hline \end{array}$

50)
$\begin{array}{r} 8 \\ \times\ 9 \\ \hline \end{array}$

51)
$\begin{array}{r} 6 \\ \times\ 10 \\ \hline \end{array}$

52)
$\begin{array}{r} 4 \\ \times\ 3 \\ \hline \end{array}$

53)
$\begin{array}{r} 5 \\ \times\ 7 \\ \hline \end{array}$

54)
$\begin{array}{r} 6 \\ \times\ 11 \\ \hline \end{array}$

55)
$\begin{array}{r} 7 \\ \times\ 1 \\ \hline \end{array}$

56)
$\begin{array}{r} 2 \\ \times\ 6 \\ \hline \end{array}$

57)
$\begin{array}{r} 0 \\ \times\ 1 \\ \hline \end{array}$

58)
$\begin{array}{r} 2 \\ \times\ 5 \\ \hline \end{array}$

59)
$\begin{array}{r} 10 \\ \times\ 7 \\ \hline \end{array}$

60)
$\begin{array}{r} 6 \\ \times\ 1 \\ \hline \end{array}$

Name: _____
Multiplying Numbers 0 to 12

Day
/100

Date: _____
Time: _____

Score
/60

1) 5 × 10

2) 6 × 5

3) 2 × 0

4) 1 × 9

5) 7 × 0

6) 7 × 11

7) 6 × 9

8) 10 × 12

9) 5 × 1

10) 10 × 7

11) 6 × 2

12) 1 × 11

13) 3 × 10

14) 9 × 12

15) 6 × 9

16) 5 × 3

17) 6 × 3

18) 6 × 9

19) 2 × 5

20) 7 × 9

21) 5 × 3

22) 0 × 8

23) 6 × 5

24) 4 × 9

25) 1 × 2

26) 8 × 10

27) 5 × 1

28) 4 × 6

29) 12 × 1

30) 4 × 9

31) 3 × 4

32) 9 × 5

33) 12 × 1

34) 5 × 9

35) 11 × 6

36) 2 × 6

37) 6 × 2

38) 6 × 11

39) 3 × 4

40) 0 × 10

41) 5 × 0

42) 0 × 2

43) 12 × 4

44) 4 × 2

45) 11 × 4

46) 1 × 6

47) 7 × 6

48) 0 × 8

49) 11 × 10

50) 3 × 5

51) 12 × 0

52) 0 × 7

53) 1 × 9

54) 0 × 4

55) 12 × 0

56) 3 × 6

57) 1 × 7

58) 8 × 11

59) 11 × 10

60) 5 × 3

Name: _____

Multiplying Numbers 0 to 12

Day /100

Date: _____
Time: _____

Score /60

1)   6
   × 5

2)   8
   × 3

3)   12
   × 8

4)   0
   × 8

5)   3
   × 8

6)   8
   × 8

7)   1
   × 5

8)   3
   × 11

9)   0
   × 9

10)   10
    × 11

11)   12
    × 8

12)   4
    × 10

13)   12
    × 7

14)   1
    × 8

15)   3
    × 7

16)   8
    × 2

17)   0
    × 9

18)   6
    × 9

19)   12
    × 10

20)   6
    × 4

21)   7
    × 9

22)   7
    × 11

23)   10
    × 6

24)   3
    × 11

25)   3
    × 0

26)   10
    × 7

27)   11
    × 0

28)   2
    × 6

29)   5
    × 10

30)   3
    × 3

31)   8
    × 0

32)   9
    × 11

33)   1
    × 6

34)   10
    × 6

35)   4
    × 0

36)   3
    × 6

37)   1
    × 5

38)   5
    × 1

39)   1
    × 6

40)   0
    × 12

41)   12
    × 4

42)   10
    × 3

43)   6
    × 1

44)   6
    × 7

45)   4
    × 5

46)   4
    × 0

47)   0
    × 4

48)   0
    × 1

49)   6
    × 1

50)   4
    × 7

51)   0
    × 10

52)   4
    × 7

53)   2
    × 5

54)   5
    × 7

55)   12
    × 7

56)   5
    × 0

57)   5
    × 10

58)   2
    × 0

59)   4
    × 10

60)   3
    × 0

Name: _____

Multiplying Numbers 0 to 12

Day /100

Date: _____

Time: _____

Score /60

1) $\begin{array}{r} 1 \\ \times\ 5 \\ \hline \end{array}$ 2) $\begin{array}{r} 0 \\ \times\ 3 \\ \hline \end{array}$ 3) $\begin{array}{r} 5 \\ \times\ 3 \\ \hline \end{array}$ 4) $\begin{array}{r} 3 \\ \times\ 1 \\ \hline \end{array}$ 5) $\begin{array}{r} 11 \\ \times\ 4 \\ \hline \end{array}$ 6) $\begin{array}{r} 5 \\ \times\ 5 \\ \hline \end{array}$

7) $\begin{array}{r} 10 \\ \times\ 7 \\ \hline \end{array}$ 8) $\begin{array}{r} 5 \\ \times\ 10 \\ \hline \end{array}$ 9) $\begin{array}{r} 10 \\ \times\ 1 \\ \hline \end{array}$ 10) $\begin{array}{r} 5 \\ \times\ 4 \\ \hline \end{array}$ 11) $\begin{array}{r} 9 \\ \times\ 6 \\ \hline \end{array}$ 12) $\begin{array}{r} 9 \\ \times\ 11 \\ \hline \end{array}$

13) $\begin{array}{r} 9 \\ \times\ 0 \\ \hline \end{array}$ 14) $\begin{array}{r} 4 \\ \times\ 11 \\ \hline \end{array}$ 15) $\begin{array}{r} 5 \\ \times\ 5 \\ \hline \end{array}$ 16) $\begin{array}{r} 3 \\ \times\ 3 \\ \hline \end{array}$ 17) $\begin{array}{r} 8 \\ \times\ 10 \\ \hline \end{array}$ 18) $\begin{array}{r} 7 \\ \times\ 12 \\ \hline \end{array}$

19) $\begin{array}{r} 1 \\ \times\ 6 \\ \hline \end{array}$ 20) $\begin{array}{r} 1 \\ \times\ 4 \\ \hline \end{array}$ 21) $\begin{array}{r} 2 \\ \times\ 7 \\ \hline \end{array}$ 22) $\begin{array}{r} 0 \\ \times\ 11 \\ \hline \end{array}$ 23) $\begin{array}{r} 8 \\ \times\ 9 \\ \hline \end{array}$ 24) $\begin{array}{r} 2 \\ \times\ 9 \\ \hline \end{array}$

25) $\begin{array}{r} 9 \\ \times\ 10 \\ \hline \end{array}$ 26) $\begin{array}{r} 10 \\ \times\ 12 \\ \hline \end{array}$ 27) $\begin{array}{r} 8 \\ \times\ 7 \\ \hline \end{array}$ 28) $\begin{array}{r} 1 \\ \times\ 12 \\ \hline \end{array}$ 29) $\begin{array}{r} 2 \\ \times\ 9 \\ \hline \end{array}$ 30) $\begin{array}{r} 1 \\ \times\ 11 \\ \hline \end{array}$

31) $\begin{array}{r} 6 \\ \times\ 10 \\ \hline \end{array}$ 32) $\begin{array}{r} 0 \\ \times\ 5 \\ \hline \end{array}$ 33) $\begin{array}{r} 3 \\ \times\ 6 \\ \hline \end{array}$ 34) $\begin{array}{r} 0 \\ \times\ 12 \\ \hline \end{array}$ 35) $\begin{array}{r} 9 \\ \times\ 8 \\ \hline \end{array}$ 36) $\begin{array}{r} 1 \\ \times\ 6 \\ \hline \end{array}$

37) $\begin{array}{r} 9 \\ \times\ 4 \\ \hline \end{array}$ 38) $\begin{array}{r} 0 \\ \times\ 12 \\ \hline \end{array}$ 39) $\begin{array}{r} 10 \\ \times\ 10 \\ \hline \end{array}$ 40) $\begin{array}{r} 1 \\ \times\ 4 \\ \hline \end{array}$ 41) $\begin{array}{r} 7 \\ \times\ 10 \\ \hline \end{array}$ 42) $\begin{array}{r} 2 \\ \times\ 11 \\ \hline \end{array}$

43) $\begin{array}{r} 6 \\ \times\ 3 \\ \hline \end{array}$ 44) $\begin{array}{r} 7 \\ \times\ 12 \\ \hline \end{array}$ 45) $\begin{array}{r} 8 \\ \times\ 1 \\ \hline \end{array}$ 46) $\begin{array}{r} 2 \\ \times\ 8 \\ \hline \end{array}$ 47) $\begin{array}{r} 12 \\ \times\ 1 \\ \hline \end{array}$ 48) $\begin{array}{r} 0 \\ \times\ 8 \\ \hline \end{array}$

49) $\begin{array}{r} 10 \\ \times\ 5 \\ \hline \end{array}$ 50) $\begin{array}{r} 8 \\ \times\ 8 \\ \hline \end{array}$ 51) $\begin{array}{r} 12 \\ \times\ 10 \\ \hline \end{array}$ 52) $\begin{array}{r} 5 \\ \times\ 5 \\ \hline \end{array}$ 53) $\begin{array}{r} 10 \\ \times\ 9 \\ \hline \end{array}$ 54) $\begin{array}{r} 6 \\ \times\ 9 \\ \hline \end{array}$

55) $\begin{array}{r} 12 \\ \times\ 7 \\ \hline \end{array}$ 56) $\begin{array}{r} 7 \\ \times\ 9 \\ \hline \end{array}$ 57) $\begin{array}{r} 0 \\ \times\ 2 \\ \hline \end{array}$ 58) $\begin{array}{r} 3 \\ \times\ 6 \\ \hline \end{array}$ 59) $\begin{array}{r} 4 \\ \times\ 0 \\ \hline \end{array}$ 60) $\begin{array}{r} 10 \\ \times\ 6 \\ \hline \end{array}$

Name: _____

Multiplying Numbers 0 to 12

Day /100

Date: _____
Time: _____

Score /60

1) 9
× 8

2) 5
× 6

3) 8
× 7

4) 6
× 10

5) 1
× 7

6) 7
× 6

7) 11
× 4

8) 9
× 8

9) 10
× 9

10) 4
× 7

11) 7
× 3

12) 8
× 2

13) 11
× 10

14) 8
× 11

15) 3
× 3

16) 4
× 6

17) 3
× 10

18) 2
× 11

19) 12
× 0

20) 0
× 11

21) 11
× 2

22) 6
× 11

23) 2
× 2

24) 8
× 6

25) 1
× 3

26) 1
× 12

27) 0
× 5

28) 8
× 6

29) 2
× 10

30) 7
× 0

31) 0
× 8

32) 6
× 6

33) 12
× 9

34) 4
× 4

35) 4
× 7

36) 7
× 8

37) 6
× 3

38) 8
× 2

39) 10
× 10

40) 1
× 5

41) 6
× 10

42) 2
× 9

43) 6
× 4

44) 1
× 9

45) 1
× 6

46) 1
× 4

47) 0
× 7

48) 10
× 0

49) 9
× 4

50) 0
× 11

51) 9
× 5

52) 3
× 7

53) 10
× 10

54) 5
× 2

55) 9
× 7

56) 2
× 1

57) 8
× 0

58) 5
× 11

59) 4
× 4

60) 0
× 3

Name: _____

Multiplying Numbers 0 to 12

Day /100

Date: _____
Time: _____

Score /60

1) $\begin{array}{r} 9 \\ \times\ 4 \\ \hline \end{array}$

2) $\begin{array}{r} 4 \\ \times\ 11 \\ \hline \end{array}$

3) $\begin{array}{r} 5 \\ \times\ 10 \\ \hline \end{array}$

4) $\begin{array}{r} 4 \\ \times\ 10 \\ \hline \end{array}$

5) $\begin{array}{r} 12 \\ \times\ 5 \\ \hline \end{array}$

6) $\begin{array}{r} 10 \\ \times\ 12 \\ \hline \end{array}$

7) $\begin{array}{r} 11 \\ \times\ 4 \\ \hline \end{array}$

8) $\begin{array}{r} 4 \\ \times\ 0 \\ \hline \end{array}$

9) $\begin{array}{r} 3 \\ \times\ 6 \\ \hline \end{array}$

10) $\begin{array}{r} 1 \\ \times\ 0 \\ \hline \end{array}$

11) $\begin{array}{r} 8 \\ \times\ 10 \\ \hline \end{array}$

12) $\begin{array}{r} 4 \\ \times\ 4 \\ \hline \end{array}$

13) $\begin{array}{r} 2 \\ \times\ 8 \\ \hline \end{array}$

14) $\begin{array}{r} 7 \\ \times\ 1 \\ \hline \end{array}$

15) $\begin{array}{r} 4 \\ \times\ 9 \\ \hline \end{array}$

16) $\begin{array}{r} 4 \\ \times\ 12 \\ \hline \end{array}$

17) $\begin{array}{r} 12 \\ \times\ 5 \\ \hline \end{array}$

18) $\begin{array}{r} 7 \\ \times\ 5 \\ \hline \end{array}$

19) $\begin{array}{r} 11 \\ \times\ 5 \\ \hline \end{array}$

20) $\begin{array}{r} 0 \\ \times\ 3 \\ \hline \end{array}$

21) $\begin{array}{r} 5 \\ \times\ 5 \\ \hline \end{array}$

22) $\begin{array}{r} 9 \\ \times\ 10 \\ \hline \end{array}$

23) $\begin{array}{r} 9 \\ \times\ 6 \\ \hline \end{array}$

24) $\begin{array}{r} 3 \\ \times\ 7 \\ \hline \end{array}$

25) $\begin{array}{r} 7 \\ \times\ 5 \\ \hline \end{array}$

26) $\begin{array}{r} 5 \\ \times\ 7 \\ \hline \end{array}$

27) $\begin{array}{r} 7 \\ \times\ 5 \\ \hline \end{array}$

28) $\begin{array}{r} 4 \\ \times\ 10 \\ \hline \end{array}$

29) $\begin{array}{r} 12 \\ \times\ 9 \\ \hline \end{array}$

30) $\begin{array}{r} 10 \\ \times\ 9 \\ \hline \end{array}$

31) $\begin{array}{r} 6 \\ \times\ 4 \\ \hline \end{array}$

32) $\begin{array}{r} 9 \\ \times\ 10 \\ \hline \end{array}$

33) $\begin{array}{r} 12 \\ \times\ 5 \\ \hline \end{array}$

34) $\begin{array}{r} 9 \\ \times\ 4 \\ \hline \end{array}$

35) $\begin{array}{r} 10 \\ \times\ 10 \\ \hline \end{array}$

36) $\begin{array}{r} 10 \\ \times\ 0 \\ \hline \end{array}$

37) $\begin{array}{r} 1 \\ \times\ 0 \\ \hline \end{array}$

38) $\begin{array}{r} 5 \\ \times\ 1 \\ \hline \end{array}$

39) $\begin{array}{r} 11 \\ \times\ 7 \\ \hline \end{array}$

40) $\begin{array}{r} 8 \\ \times\ 1 \\ \hline \end{array}$

41) $\begin{array}{r} 11 \\ \times\ 8 \\ \hline \end{array}$

42) $\begin{array}{r} 2 \\ \times\ 1 \\ \hline \end{array}$

43) $\begin{array}{r} 7 \\ \times\ 8 \\ \hline \end{array}$

44) $\begin{array}{r} 8 \\ \times\ 11 \\ \hline \end{array}$

45) $\begin{array}{r} 12 \\ \times\ 6 \\ \hline \end{array}$

46) $\begin{array}{r} 1 \\ \times\ 4 \\ \hline \end{array}$

47) $\begin{array}{r} 4 \\ \times\ 7 \\ \hline \end{array}$

48) $\begin{array}{r} 4 \\ \times\ 4 \\ \hline \end{array}$

49) $\begin{array}{r} 4 \\ \times\ 8 \\ \hline \end{array}$

50) $\begin{array}{r} 8 \\ \times\ 6 \\ \hline \end{array}$

51) $\begin{array}{r} 2 \\ \times\ 3 \\ \hline \end{array}$

52) $\begin{array}{r} 0 \\ \times\ 1 \\ \hline \end{array}$

53) $\begin{array}{r} 5 \\ \times\ 1 \\ \hline \end{array}$

54) $\begin{array}{r} 5 \\ \times\ 11 \\ \hline \end{array}$

55) $\begin{array}{r} 11 \\ \times\ 3 \\ \hline \end{array}$

56) $\begin{array}{r} 3 \\ \times\ 3 \\ \hline \end{array}$

57) $\begin{array}{r} 9 \\ \times\ 1 \\ \hline \end{array}$

58) $\begin{array}{r} 10 \\ \times\ 1 \\ \hline \end{array}$

59) $\begin{array}{r} 2 \\ \times\ 5 \\ \hline \end{array}$

60) $\begin{array}{r} 1 \\ \times\ 9 \\ \hline \end{array}$

Name: _____

Multiplying Numbers 0 to 12

Day /100

Date: _____

Time: _____

Score /60

1)   1
 × 3

2)   5
 × 6

3)   9
 × 0

4)   2
 × 8

5)   0
 × 5

6)   4
 × 1

7)   11
 × 10

8)   6
 × 5

9)   9
 × 4

10)   10
 × 12

11)   4
 × 1

12)   10
 × 12

13)   10
 × 2

14)   6
 × 0

15)   4
 × 10

16)   3
 × 4

17)   12
 × 7

18)   6
 × 8

19)   0
 × 3

20)   10
 × 11

21)   4
 × 8

22)   10
 × 12

23)   2
 × 6

24)   5
 × 8

25)   3
 × 10

26)   3
 × 11

27)   7
 × 7

28)   1
 × 12

29)   9
 × 4

30)   8
 × 7

31)   0
 × 10

32)   10
 × 0

33)   10
 × 6

34)   6
 × 6

35)   8
 × 2

36)   0
 × 3

37)   4
 × 3

38)   6
 × 4

39)   8
 × 8

40)   0
 × 8

41)   5
 × 4

42)   6
 × 11

43)   2
 × 4

44)   0
 × 6

45)   3
 × 1

46)   4
 × 4

47)   6
 × 6

48)   6
 × 2

49)   10
 × 3

50)   7
 × 4

51)   7
 × 10

52)   4
 × 8

53)   7
 × 10

54)   8
 × 8

55)   5
 × 9

56)   6
 × 7

57)   4
 × 2

58)   3
 × 1

59)   2
 × 7

60)   10
 × 9

Name: _____

Multiplying Numbers 0 to 12

Day
/100

Date: _____
Time: _____

Score
/60

1) $\begin{array}{r} 6 \\ \times\ 3 \\ \hline \end{array}$

2) $\begin{array}{r} 9 \\ \times\ 9 \\ \hline \end{array}$

3) $\begin{array}{r} 5 \\ \times\ 5 \\ \hline \end{array}$

4) $\begin{array}{r} 10 \\ \times\ 3 \\ \hline \end{array}$

5) $\begin{array}{r} 11 \\ \times\ 0 \\ \hline \end{array}$

6) $\begin{array}{r} 3 \\ \times\ 11 \\ \hline \end{array}$

7) $\begin{array}{r} 2 \\ \times\ 3 \\ \hline \end{array}$

8) $\begin{array}{r} 1 \\ \times\ 0 \\ \hline \end{array}$

9) $\begin{array}{r} 4 \\ \times\ 0 \\ \hline \end{array}$

10) $\begin{array}{r} 4 \\ \times\ 4 \\ \hline \end{array}$

11) $\begin{array}{r} 6 \\ \times\ 0 \\ \hline \end{array}$

12) $\begin{array}{r} 3 \\ \times\ 12 \\ \hline \end{array}$

13) $\begin{array}{r} 0 \\ \times\ 9 \\ \hline \end{array}$

14) $\begin{array}{r} 6 \\ \times\ 12 \\ \hline \end{array}$

15) $\begin{array}{r} 7 \\ \times\ 8 \\ \hline \end{array}$

16) $\begin{array}{r} 1 \\ \times\ 11 \\ \hline \end{array}$

17) $\begin{array}{r} 5 \\ \times\ 2 \\ \hline \end{array}$

18) $\begin{array}{r} 6 \\ \times\ 6 \\ \hline \end{array}$

19) $\begin{array}{r} 2 \\ \times\ 0 \\ \hline \end{array}$

20) $\begin{array}{r} 4 \\ \times\ 3 \\ \hline \end{array}$

21) $\begin{array}{r} 4 \\ \times\ 9 \\ \hline \end{array}$

22) $\begin{array}{r} 3 \\ \times\ 0 \\ \hline \end{array}$

23) $\begin{array}{r} 7 \\ \times\ 6 \\ \hline \end{array}$

24) $\begin{array}{r} 2 \\ \times\ 4 \\ \hline \end{array}$

25) $\begin{array}{r} 6 \\ \times\ 5 \\ \hline \end{array}$

26) $\begin{array}{r} 9 \\ \times\ 6 \\ \hline \end{array}$

27) $\begin{array}{r} 10 \\ \times\ 3 \\ \hline \end{array}$

28) $\begin{array}{r} 2 \\ \times\ 3 \\ \hline \end{array}$

29) $\begin{array}{r} 10 \\ \times\ 9 \\ \hline \end{array}$

30) $\begin{array}{r} 6 \\ \times\ 11 \\ \hline \end{array}$

31) $\begin{array}{r} 3 \\ \times\ 2 \\ \hline \end{array}$

32) $\begin{array}{r} 1 \\ \times\ 0 \\ \hline \end{array}$

33) $\begin{array}{r} 11 \\ \times\ 10 \\ \hline \end{array}$

34) $\begin{array}{r} 7 \\ \times\ 4 \\ \hline \end{array}$

35) $\begin{array}{r} 7 \\ \times\ 5 \\ \hline \end{array}$

36) $\begin{array}{r} 3 \\ \times\ 4 \\ \hline \end{array}$

37) $\begin{array}{r} 0 \\ \times\ 8 \\ \hline \end{array}$

38) $\begin{array}{r} 9 \\ \times\ 7 \\ \hline \end{array}$

39) $\begin{array}{r} 9 \\ \times\ 7 \\ \hline \end{array}$

40) $\begin{array}{r} 1 \\ \times\ 8 \\ \hline \end{array}$

41) $\begin{array}{r} 9 \\ \times\ 10 \\ \hline \end{array}$

42) $\begin{array}{r} 8 \\ \times\ 1 \\ \hline \end{array}$

43) $\begin{array}{r} 5 \\ \times\ 10 \\ \hline \end{array}$

44) $\begin{array}{r} 6 \\ \times\ 7 \\ \hline \end{array}$

45) $\begin{array}{r} 0 \\ \times\ 2 \\ \hline \end{array}$

46) $\begin{array}{r} 3 \\ \times\ 5 \\ \hline \end{array}$

47) $\begin{array}{r} 10 \\ \times\ 8 \\ \hline \end{array}$

48) $\begin{array}{r} 6 \\ \times\ 8 \\ \hline \end{array}$

49) $\begin{array}{r} 4 \\ \times\ 6 \\ \hline \end{array}$

50) $\begin{array}{r} 10 \\ \times\ 8 \\ \hline \end{array}$

51) $\begin{array}{r} 5 \\ \times\ 3 \\ \hline \end{array}$

52) $\begin{array}{r} 0 \\ \times\ 11 \\ \hline \end{array}$

53) $\begin{array}{r} 3 \\ \times\ 6 \\ \hline \end{array}$

54) $\begin{array}{r} 4 \\ \times\ 9 \\ \hline \end{array}$

55) $\begin{array}{r} 11 \\ \times\ 8 \\ \hline \end{array}$

56) $\begin{array}{r} 5 \\ \times\ 2 \\ \hline \end{array}$

57) $\begin{array}{r} 8 \\ \times\ 0 \\ \hline \end{array}$

58) $\begin{array}{r} 3 \\ \times\ 8 \\ \hline \end{array}$

59) $\begin{array}{r} 10 \\ \times\ 2 \\ \hline \end{array}$

60) $\begin{array}{r} 4 \\ \times\ 6 \\ \hline \end{array}$

Name: _____

Multiplying Numbers 0 to 12

Day /100

Date: _____
Time: _____

Score /60

1) 11
  × 9

2)   6
  × 8

3)   7
  × 0

4)   9
  × 0

5)   0
  × 0

6)   5
  × 3

7)   4
  × 1

8)   2
  × 0

9)   2
  × 9

10)   0
  × 7

11) 12
  × 6

12)   2
  × 5

13)   1
  × 7

14)   7
  × 3

15)   4
  × 6

16)   8
  × 3

17)   5
  × 3

18)   8
  × 7

19)   7
  × 0

20)   5
  × 1

21)   6
  × 6

22)   5
  × 2

23)   9
  × 5

24)   2
  × 1

25) 11
  × 8

26)   0
  × 0

27)   0
  × 10

28)   9
  × 0

29)   0
  × 2

30)   1
  × 4

31) 10
  × 10

32)   2
  × 2

33)   0
  × 3

34)   9
  × 9

35)   3
  × 4

36)   6
  × 5

37)   1
  × 4

38)   9
  × 7

39)   9
  × 10

40)   4
  × 1

41)   1
  × 2

42)   8
  × 4

43) 10
  × 10

44)   9
  × 6

45)   1
  × 4

46)   0
  × 9

47)   0
  × 6

48)   6
  × 0

49)   3
  × 8

50)   3
  × 2

51)   8
  × 3

52) 10
  × 12

53)   1
  × 5

54)   2
  × 4

55) 11
  × 0

56)   9
  × 11

57)   2
  × 0

58)   8
  × 1

59)   8
  × 6

60)   6
  × 8

Name: _____

Multiplying Numbers 0 to 12

Day /100

Date: _____
Time: _____

Score /60

1) $\begin{array}{r} 11 \\ \times\ 6 \\ \hline \end{array}$
2) $\begin{array}{r} 6 \\ \times\ 2 \\ \hline \end{array}$
3) $\begin{array}{r} 5 \\ \times\ 0 \\ \hline \end{array}$
4) $\begin{array}{r} 6 \\ \times\ 0 \\ \hline \end{array}$
5) $\begin{array}{r} 10 \\ \times\ 5 \\ \hline \end{array}$
6) $\begin{array}{r} 7 \\ \times\ 7 \\ \hline \end{array}$

7) $\begin{array}{r} 4 \\ \times\ 4 \\ \hline \end{array}$
8) $\begin{array}{r} 0 \\ \times\ 7 \\ \hline \end{array}$
9) $\begin{array}{r} 7 \\ \times\ 9 \\ \hline \end{array}$
10) $\begin{array}{r} 3 \\ \times\ 4 \\ \hline \end{array}$
11) $\begin{array}{r} 5 \\ \times\ 3 \\ \hline \end{array}$
12) $\begin{array}{r} 2 \\ \times\ 3 \\ \hline \end{array}$

13) $\begin{array}{r} 0 \\ \times\ 7 \\ \hline \end{array}$
14) $\begin{array}{r} 3 \\ \times\ 7 \\ \hline \end{array}$
15) $\begin{array}{r} 4 \\ \times\ 10 \\ \hline \end{array}$
16) $\begin{array}{r} 7 \\ \times\ 8 \\ \hline \end{array}$
17) $\begin{array}{r} 7 \\ \times\ 9 \\ \hline \end{array}$
18) $\begin{array}{r} 7 \\ \times\ 3 \\ \hline \end{array}$

19) $\begin{array}{r} 11 \\ \times\ 0 \\ \hline \end{array}$
20) $\begin{array}{r} 6 \\ \times\ 6 \\ \hline \end{array}$
21) $\begin{array}{r} 9 \\ \times\ 3 \\ \hline \end{array}$
22) $\begin{array}{r} 10 \\ \times\ 3 \\ \hline \end{array}$
23) $\begin{array}{r} 12 \\ \times\ 1 \\ \hline \end{array}$
24) $\begin{array}{r} 0 \\ \times\ 1 \\ \hline \end{array}$

25) $\begin{array}{r} 8 \\ \times\ 10 \\ \hline \end{array}$
26) $\begin{array}{r} 8 \\ \times\ 3 \\ \hline \end{array}$
27) $\begin{array}{r} 2 \\ \times\ 0 \\ \hline \end{array}$
28) $\begin{array}{r} 8 \\ \times\ 8 \\ \hline \end{array}$
29) $\begin{array}{r} 8 \\ \times\ 8 \\ \hline \end{array}$
30) $\begin{array}{r} 4 \\ \times\ 12 \\ \hline \end{array}$

31) $\begin{array}{r} 12 \\ \times\ 10 \\ \hline \end{array}$
32) $\begin{array}{r} 9 \\ \times\ 12 \\ \hline \end{array}$
33) $\begin{array}{r} 4 \\ \times\ 3 \\ \hline \end{array}$
34) $\begin{array}{r} 3 \\ \times\ 4 \\ \hline \end{array}$
35) $\begin{array}{r} 12 \\ \times\ 10 \\ \hline \end{array}$
36) $\begin{array}{r} 3 \\ \times\ 3 \\ \hline \end{array}$

37) $\begin{array}{r} 1 \\ \times\ 5 \\ \hline \end{array}$
38) $\begin{array}{r} 7 \\ \times\ 4 \\ \hline \end{array}$
39) $\begin{array}{r} 4 \\ \times\ 5 \\ \hline \end{array}$
40) $\begin{array}{r} 1 \\ \times\ 10 \\ \hline \end{array}$
41) $\begin{array}{r} 5 \\ \times\ 7 \\ \hline \end{array}$
42) $\begin{array}{r} 3 \\ \times\ 10 \\ \hline \end{array}$

43) $\begin{array}{r} 0 \\ \times\ 6 \\ \hline \end{array}$
44) $\begin{array}{r} 7 \\ \times\ 5 \\ \hline \end{array}$
45) $\begin{array}{r} 11 \\ \times\ 0 \\ \hline \end{array}$
46) $\begin{array}{r} 4 \\ \times\ 8 \\ \hline \end{array}$
47) $\begin{array}{r} 4 \\ \times\ 1 \\ \hline \end{array}$
48) $\begin{array}{r} 6 \\ \times\ 7 \\ \hline \end{array}$

49) $\begin{array}{r} 6 \\ \times\ 6 \\ \hline \end{array}$
50) $\begin{array}{r} 10 \\ \times\ 8 \\ \hline \end{array}$
51) $\begin{array}{r} 7 \\ \times\ 4 \\ \hline \end{array}$
52) $\begin{array}{r} 6 \\ \times\ 6 \\ \hline \end{array}$
53) $\begin{array}{r} 5 \\ \times\ 2 \\ \hline \end{array}$
54) $\begin{array}{r} 0 \\ \times\ 11 \\ \hline \end{array}$

55) $\begin{array}{r} 0 \\ \times\ 3 \\ \hline \end{array}$
56) $\begin{array}{r} 2 \\ \times\ 2 \\ \hline \end{array}$
57) $\begin{array}{r} 6 \\ \times\ 10 \\ \hline \end{array}$
58) $\begin{array}{r} 6 \\ \times\ 1 \\ \hline \end{array}$
59) $\begin{array}{r} 9 \\ \times\ 10 \\ \hline \end{array}$
60) $\begin{array}{r} 6 \\ \times\ 11 \\ \hline \end{array}$

1) 6 × 3

2) 6 × 10

3) 11 × 2

4) 8 × 11

5) 4 × 5

6) 1 × 0

7) 10 × 10

8) 2 × 11

9) 8 × 3

10) 8 × 8

11) 10 × 8

12) 9 × 2

13) 0 × 0

14) 6 × 2

15) 0 × 2

16) 4 × 5

17) 0 × 1

18) 6 × 3

19) 0 × 1

20) 1 × 1

21) 6 × 9

22) 3 × 9

23) 0 × 6

24) 0 × 7

25) 10 × 3

26) 0 × 6

27) 12 × 5

28) 6 × 6

29) 12 × 1

30) 6 × 9

31) 3 × 0

32) 3 × 8

33) 9 × 10

34) 7 × 10

35) 12 × 7

36) 9 × 9

37) 0 × 8

38) 9 × 4

39) 1 × 5

40) 9 × 5

41) 2 × 5

42) 8 × 4

43) 8 × 1

44) 3 × 12

45) 1 × 8

46) 5 × 10

47) 2 × 2

48) 7 × 4

49) 4 × 5

50) 1 × 9

51) 4 × 0

52) 2 × 9

53) 6 × 6

54) 3 × 0

55) 10 × 6

56) 3 × 10

57) 10 × 3

58) 2 × 4

59) 12 × 1

60) 1 × 4

Name: _____

Multiplying Numbers 0 to 12

Day /100

Date: _____

Time: _____

Score /60

1) 7 × 8

2) 10 × 4

3) 1 × 3

4) 8 × 12

5) 3 × 9

6) 2 × 9

7) 6 × 4

8) 10 × 9

9) 12 × 0

10) 4 × 12

11) 6 × 5

12) 5 × 3

13) 0 × 1

14) 0 × 7

15) 9 × 1

16) 8 × 1

17) 7 × 10

18) 2 × 8

19) 1 × 3

20) 8 × 2

21) 5 × 10

22) 1 × 10

23) 5 × 10

24) 8 × 11

25) 12 × 10

26) 9 × 4

27) 10 × 6

28) 5 × 1

29) 9 × 1

30) 7 × 11

31) 4 × 10

32) 5 × 8

33) 10 × 4

34) 5 × 4

35) 3 × 10

36) 10 × 1

37) 0 × 5

38) 0 × 12

39) 3 × 7

40) 6 × 1

41) 9 × 1

42) 7 × 8

43) 0 × 1

44) 4 × 2

45) 10 × 5

46) 0 × 7

47) 8 × 4

48) 5 × 12

49) 2 × 4

50) 2 × 1

51) 10 × 3

52) 3 × 8

53) 4 × 0

54) 10 × 5

55) 9 × 1

56) 9 × 7

57) 2 × 8

58) 7 × 4

59) 4 × 9

60) 4 × 9

Name: _____

Multiplying Numbers 0 to 12

Day /100

Date: _____

Time: _____

Score /60

1) 5 × 8

2) 1 × 7

3) 7 × 5

4) 6 × 6

5) 10 × 1

6) 10 × 5

7) 11 × 3

8) 1 × 5

9) 4 × 4

10) 4 × 0

11) 6 × 0

12) 4 × 8

13) 9 × 5

14) 8 × 0

15) 11 × 6

16) 10 × 11

17) 1 × 5

18) 2 × 12

19) 10 × 10

20) 9 × 11

21) 1 × 6

22) 2 × 6

23) 2 × 3

24) 6 × 9

25) 0 × 10

26) 0 × 10

27) 9 × 3

28) 6 × 5

29) 8 × 9

30) 6 × 12

31) 4 × 9

32) 9 × 5

33) 11 × 10

34) 0 × 12

35) 4 × 2

36) 10 × 6

37) 12 × 10

38) 7 × 9

39) 12 × 2

40) 4 × 5

41) 0 × 7

42) 7 × 11

43) 4 × 9

44) 9 × 10

45) 4 × 7

46) 7 × 11

47) 1 × 5

48) 7 × 4

49) 3 × 2

50) 4 × 12

51) 10 × 6

52) 8 × 8

53) 6 × 10

54) 8 × 11

55) 2 × 1

56) 3 × 9

57) 8 × 7

58) 10 × 0

59) 0 × 1

60) 8 × 7

Name: _____

Multiplying Numbers 0 to 12

Day /100

Date: _____

Time: _____

Score /60

1) $\begin{array}{r} 9 \\ \times\ 6 \\ \hline \end{array}$

2) $\begin{array}{r} 7 \\ \times\ 6 \\ \hline \end{array}$

3) $\begin{array}{r} 0 \\ \times\ 8 \\ \hline \end{array}$

4) $\begin{array}{r} 2 \\ \times\ 12 \\ \hline \end{array}$

5) $\begin{array}{r} 4 \\ \times\ 0 \\ \hline \end{array}$

6) $\begin{array}{r} 10 \\ \times\ 1 \\ \hline \end{array}$

7) $\begin{array}{r} 7 \\ \times\ 7 \\ \hline \end{array}$

8) $\begin{array}{r} 8 \\ \times\ 4 \\ \hline \end{array}$

9) $\begin{array}{r} 2 \\ \times\ 8 \\ \hline \end{array}$

10) $\begin{array}{r} 1 \\ \times\ 6 \\ \hline \end{array}$

11) $\begin{array}{r} 4 \\ \times\ 6 \\ \hline \end{array}$

12) $\begin{array}{r} 1 \\ \times\ 11 \\ \hline \end{array}$

13) $\begin{array}{r} 2 \\ \times\ 9 \\ \hline \end{array}$

14) $\begin{array}{r} 3 \\ \times\ 0 \\ \hline \end{array}$

15) $\begin{array}{r} 8 \\ \times\ 9 \\ \hline \end{array}$

16) $\begin{array}{r} 10 \\ \times\ 6 \\ \hline \end{array}$

17) $\begin{array}{r} 11 \\ \times\ 10 \\ \hline \end{array}$

18) $\begin{array}{r} 0 \\ \times\ 2 \\ \hline \end{array}$

19) $\begin{array}{r} 3 \\ \times\ 7 \\ \hline \end{array}$

20) $\begin{array}{r} 0 \\ \times\ 12 \\ \hline \end{array}$

21) $\begin{array}{r} 12 \\ \times\ 3 \\ \hline \end{array}$

22) $\begin{array}{r} 5 \\ \times\ 9 \\ \hline \end{array}$

23) $\begin{array}{r} 11 \\ \times\ 4 \\ \hline \end{array}$

24) $\begin{array}{r} 4 \\ \times\ 0 \\ \hline \end{array}$

25) $\begin{array}{r} 8 \\ \times\ 10 \\ \hline \end{array}$

26) $\begin{array}{r} 4 \\ \times\ 0 \\ \hline \end{array}$

27) $\begin{array}{r} 7 \\ \times\ 6 \\ \hline \end{array}$

28) $\begin{array}{r} 1 \\ \times\ 6 \\ \hline \end{array}$

29) $\begin{array}{r} 9 \\ \times\ 0 \\ \hline \end{array}$

30) $\begin{array}{r} 2 \\ \times\ 6 \\ \hline \end{array}$

31) $\begin{array}{r} 11 \\ \times\ 9 \\ \hline \end{array}$

32) $\begin{array}{r} 3 \\ \times\ 0 \\ \hline \end{array}$

33) $\begin{array}{r} 1 \\ \times\ 6 \\ \hline \end{array}$

34) $\begin{array}{r} 5 \\ \times\ 8 \\ \hline \end{array}$

35) $\begin{array}{r} 11 \\ \times\ 7 \\ \hline \end{array}$

36) $\begin{array}{r} 8 \\ \times\ 0 \\ \hline \end{array}$

37) $\begin{array}{r} 2 \\ \times\ 8 \\ \hline \end{array}$

38) $\begin{array}{r} 10 \\ \times\ 11 \\ \hline \end{array}$

39) $\begin{array}{r} 7 \\ \times\ 6 \\ \hline \end{array}$

40) $\begin{array}{r} 4 \\ \times\ 1 \\ \hline \end{array}$

41) $\begin{array}{r} 10 \\ \times\ 1 \\ \hline \end{array}$

42) $\begin{array}{r} 3 \\ \times\ 7 \\ \hline \end{array}$

43) $\begin{array}{r} 5 \\ \times\ 7 \\ \hline \end{array}$

44) $\begin{array}{r} 8 \\ \times\ 9 \\ \hline \end{array}$

45) $\begin{array}{r} 7 \\ \times\ 0 \\ \hline \end{array}$

46) $\begin{array}{r} 8 \\ \times\ 8 \\ \hline \end{array}$

47) $\begin{array}{r} 0 \\ \times\ 3 \\ \hline \end{array}$

48) $\begin{array}{r} 5 \\ \times\ 9 \\ \hline \end{array}$

49) $\begin{array}{r} 1 \\ \times\ 1 \\ \hline \end{array}$

50) $\begin{array}{r} 4 \\ \times\ 4 \\ \hline \end{array}$

51) $\begin{array}{r} 9 \\ \times\ 0 \\ \hline \end{array}$

52) $\begin{array}{r} 1 \\ \times\ 0 \\ \hline \end{array}$

53) $\begin{array}{r} 3 \\ \times\ 1 \\ \hline \end{array}$

54) $\begin{array}{r} 3 \\ \times\ 2 \\ \hline \end{array}$

55) $\begin{array}{r} 4 \\ \times\ 5 \\ \hline \end{array}$

56) $\begin{array}{r} 5 \\ \times\ 2 \\ \hline \end{array}$

57) $\begin{array}{r} 2 \\ \times\ 2 \\ \hline \end{array}$

58) $\begin{array}{r} 3 \\ \times\ 6 \\ \hline \end{array}$

59) $\begin{array}{r} 1 \\ \times\ 8 \\ \hline \end{array}$

60) $\begin{array}{r} 5 \\ \times\ 4 \\ \hline \end{array}$

Multiplying Numbers 0 to 12

Time: _____

1)
$$\begin{array}{r} 6 \\ \times\ 7 \\ \hline \end{array}$$

2)
$$\begin{array}{r} 10 \\ \times\ 11 \\ \hline \end{array}$$

3)
$$\begin{array}{r} 8 \\ \times\ 1 \\ \hline \end{array}$$

4)
$$\begin{array}{r} 9 \\ \times\ 11 \\ \hline \end{array}$$

5)
$$\begin{array}{r} 11 \\ \times\ 10 \\ \hline \end{array}$$

6)
$$\begin{array}{r} 0 \\ \times\ 9 \\ \hline \end{array}$$

7)
$$\begin{array}{r} 8 \\ \times\ 10 \\ \hline \end{array}$$

8)
$$\begin{array}{r} 2 \\ \times\ 8 \\ \hline \end{array}$$

9)
$$\begin{array}{r} 0 \\ \times\ 1 \\ \hline \end{array}$$

10)
$$\begin{array}{r} 9 \\ \times\ 0 \\ \hline \end{array}$$

11)
$$\begin{array}{r} 2 \\ \times\ 2 \\ \hline \end{array}$$

12)
$$\begin{array}{r} 10 \\ \times\ 10 \\ \hline \end{array}$$

13)
$$\begin{array}{r} 3 \\ \times\ 2 \\ \hline \end{array}$$

14)
$$\begin{array}{r} 3 \\ \times\ 8 \\ \hline \end{array}$$

15)
$$\begin{array}{r} 7 \\ \times\ 1 \\ \hline \end{array}$$

16)
$$\begin{array}{r} 5 \\ \times\ 5 \\ \hline \end{array}$$

17)
$$\begin{array}{r} 2 \\ \times\ 9 \\ \hline \end{array}$$

18)
$$\begin{array}{r} 4 \\ \times\ 9 \\ \hline \end{array}$$

19)
$$\begin{array}{r} 8 \\ \times\ 0 \\ \hline \end{array}$$

20)
$$\begin{array}{r} 9 \\ \times\ 11 \\ \hline \end{array}$$

21)
$$\begin{array}{r} 12 \\ \times\ 1 \\ \hline \end{array}$$

22)
$$\begin{array}{r} 2 \\ \times\ 6 \\ \hline \end{array}$$

23)
$$\begin{array}{r} 2 \\ \times\ 6 \\ \hline \end{array}$$

24)
$$\begin{array}{r} 3 \\ \times\ 2 \\ \hline \end{array}$$

25)
$$\begin{array}{r} 3 \\ \times\ 2 \\ \hline \end{array}$$

26)
$$\begin{array}{r} 6 \\ \times\ 0 \\ \hline \end{array}$$

27)
$$\begin{array}{r} 1 \\ \times\ 9 \\ \hline \end{array}$$

28)
$$\begin{array}{r} 9 \\ \times\ 11 \\ \hline \end{array}$$

29)
$$\begin{array}{r} 3 \\ \times\ 2 \\ \hline \end{array}$$

30)
$$\begin{array}{r} 10 \\ \times\ 5 \\ \hline \end{array}$$

31)
$$\begin{array}{r} 6 \\ \times\ 9 \\ \hline \end{array}$$

32)
$$\begin{array}{r} 2 \\ \times\ 8 \\ \hline \end{array}$$

33)
$$\begin{array}{r} 3 \\ \times\ 5 \\ \hline \end{array}$$

34)
$$\begin{array}{r} 2 \\ \times\ 8 \\ \hline \end{array}$$

35)
$$\begin{array}{r} 4 \\ \times\ 8 \\ \hline \end{array}$$

36)
$$\begin{array}{r} 3 \\ \times\ 3 \\ \hline \end{array}$$

37)
$$\begin{array}{r} 6 \\ \times\ 3 \\ \hline \end{array}$$

38)
$$\begin{array}{r} 2 \\ \times\ 5 \\ \hline \end{array}$$

39)
$$\begin{array}{r} 4 \\ \times\ 10 \\ \hline \end{array}$$

40)
$$\begin{array}{r} 10 \\ \times\ 12 \\ \hline \end{array}$$

41)
$$\begin{array}{r} 5 \\ \times\ 9 \\ \hline \end{array}$$

42)
$$\begin{array}{r} 5 \\ \times\ 9 \\ \hline \end{array}$$

43)
$$\begin{array}{r} 7 \\ \times\ 6 \\ \hline \end{array}$$

44)
$$\begin{array}{r} 6 \\ \times\ 2 \\ \hline \end{array}$$

45)
$$\begin{array}{r} 8 \\ \times\ 8 \\ \hline \end{array}$$

46)
$$\begin{array}{r} 7 \\ \times\ 4 \\ \hline \end{array}$$

47)
$$\begin{array}{r} 9 \\ \times\ 10 \\ \hline \end{array}$$

48)
$$\begin{array}{r} 10 \\ \times\ 4 \\ \hline \end{array}$$

49)
$$\begin{array}{r} 2 \\ \times\ 9 \\ \hline \end{array}$$

50)
$$\begin{array}{r} 7 \\ \times\ 1 \\ \hline \end{array}$$

51)
$$\begin{array}{r} 8 \\ \times\ 10 \\ \hline \end{array}$$

52)
$$\begin{array}{r} 1 \\ \times\ 12 \\ \hline \end{array}$$

53)
$$\begin{array}{r} 9 \\ \times\ 5 \\ \hline \end{array}$$

54)
$$\begin{array}{r} 8 \\ \times\ 9 \\ \hline \end{array}$$

55)
$$\begin{array}{r} 5 \\ \times\ 5 \\ \hline \end{array}$$

56)
$$\begin{array}{r} 10 \\ \times\ 2 \\ \hline \end{array}$$

57)
$$\begin{array}{r} 4 \\ \times\ 4 \\ \hline \end{array}$$

58)
$$\begin{array}{r} 1 \\ \times\ 12 \\ \hline \end{array}$$

59)
$$\begin{array}{r} 0 \\ \times\ 1 \\ \hline \end{array}$$

60)
$$\begin{array}{r} 5 \\ \times\ 11 \\ \hline \end{array}$$

Page 1, Item 1:
(1)0 (2)7 (3)5 (4)4 (5)0 (6)0 (7)0 (8)2 (9)0
(10)7 (11)0 (12)3 (13)3 (14)0 (15)0 (16)3
(17)0 (18)1 (19)8 (20)0 (21)5 (22)5 (23)0
(24)8 (25)0 (26)0 (27)0 (28)0 (29)0 (30)0
(31)0 (32)2 (33)0 (34)3 (35)7 (36)0 (37)0
(38)4 (39)3 (40)2 (41)0 (42)6 (43)4 (44)2
(45)0 (46)0 (47)1 (48)0 (49)0 (50)2 (51)0
(52)0 (53)7 (54)0 (55)0 (56)8 (57)0 (58)0
(59)0 (60)0
Page 2, Item 1:
(1)3 (2)0 (3)0 (4)0 (5)0 (6)0 (7)5 (8)0 (9)3
(10)9 (11)0 (12)6 (13)2 (14)4 (15)6 (16)5
(17)0 (18)8 (19)0 (20)0 (21)0 (22)9 (23)0
(24)5 (25)0 (26)0 (27)8 (28)6 (29)9 (30)0
(31)0 (32)4 (33)6 (34)5 (35)0 (36)7 (37)0
(38)0 (39)0 (40)1 (41)0 (42)0 (43)4 (44)0
(45)0 (46)3 (47)8 (48)9 (49)4 (50)3 (51)8
(52)0 (53)0 (54)0 (55)7 (56)2 (57)3 (58)2
(59)3 (60)3
Page 3, Item 1:
(1)2 (2)1 (3)9 (4)0 (5)0 (6)0 (7)1 (8)0 (9)0
(10)0 (11)0 (12)0 (13)4 (14)0 (15)0 (16)0
(17)0 (18)9 (19)7 (20)0 (21)6 (22)0 (23)7
(24)0 (25)0 (26)0 (27)0 (28)3 (29)4 (30)0
(31)0 (32)8 (33)1 (34)0 (35)0 (36)3 (37)0
(38)0 (39)8 (40)0 (41)6 (42)3 (43)0 (44)0
(45)0 (46)6 (47)0 (48)0 (49)0 (50)7 (51)0
(52)0 (53)0 (54)8 (55)0 (56)5 (57)0 (58)6
(59)0 (60)4
Page 4, Item 1:
(1)0 (2)4 (3)8 (4)0 (5)1 (6)5 (7)0 (8)0 (9)6
(10)0 (11)0 (12)0 (13)0 (14)0 (15)8 (16)0
(17)0 (18)0 (19)0 (20)3 (21)3 (22)0 (23)0
(24)4 (25)6 (26)8 (27)0 (28)0 (29)7 (30)4
(31)0 (32)0 (33)0 (34)0 (35)6 (36)0 (37)0
(38)0 (39)0 (40)0 (41)0 (42)7 (43)2 (44)0
(45)4 (46)2 (47)0 (48)0 (49)0 (50)0 (51)0
(52)4 (53)9 (54)0 (55)0 (56)8 (57)5 (58)4
(59)4 (60)3

Page 5, Item 1:
(1)0 (2)0 (3)0 (4)5 (5)0 (6)5 (7)0 (8)0 (9)0
(10)5 (11)8 (12)8 (13)6 (14)0 (15)6 (16)1
(17)4 (18)7 (19)8 (20)9 (21)0 (22)7 (23)0
(24)0 (25)2 (26)3 (27)0 (28)9 (29)8 (30)1
(31)2 (32)7 (33)7 (34)1 (35)0 (36)0 (37)5
(38)7 (39)0 (40)6 (41)0 (42)9 (43)0 (44)0
(45)6 (46)1 (47)9 (48)2 (49)3 (50)0 (51)6
(52)1 (53)2 (54)0 (55)0 (56)0 (57)0 (58)0
(59)5 (60)3

Page 6, Item 1:
(1)6 (2)2 (3)18 (4)18 (5)0 (6)16 (7)0 (8)4
(9)6 (10)10 (11)12 (12)12 (13)14 (14)14
(15)14 (16)12 (17)16 (18)2 (19)4 (20)0
(21)6 (22)18 (23)4 (24)16 (25)2 (26)8 (27)0
(28)2 (29)8 (30)10 (31)16 (32)4 (33)4
(34)10 (35)6 (36)18 (37)18 (38)16 (39)2
(40)12 (41)2 (42)0 (43)18 (44)18 (45)10
(46)8 (47)4 (48)12 (49)8 (50)10 (51)16
(52)16 (53)2 (54)4 (55)10 (56)18 (57)4
(58)12 (59)4 (60)4
Page 7, Item 1:
(1)14 (2)6 (3)10 (4)0 (5)2 (6)16 (7)16 (8)2
(9)14 (10)12 (11)10 (12)6 (13)10 (14)2
(15)10 (16)12 (17)12 (18)4 (19)14 (20)10
(21)14 (22)6 (23)0 (24)12 (25)10 (26)10
(27)4 (28)16 (29)12 (30)4 (31)12 (32)18
(33)2 (34)6 (35)12 (36)10 (37)10 (38)18
(39)0 (40)0 (41)6 (42)4 (43)10 (44)4 (45)14
(46)8 (47)2 (48)18 (49)10 (50)2 (51)14
(52)8 (53)18 (54)16 (55)18 (56)0 (57)18
(58)6 (59)2 (60)8
Page 8, Item 1:
(1)10 (2)8 (3)8 (4)0 (5)0 (6)10 (7)8 (8)6 (9)2
(10)8 (11)2 (12)6 (13)6 (14)18 (15)10 (16)8
(17)8 (18)4 (19)6 (20)10 (21)2 (22)14 (23)8
(24)18 (25)2 (26)4 (27)8 (28)6 (29)8 (30)12
(31)14 (32)12 (33)8 (34)12 (35)6 (36)16
(37)12 (38)10 (39)10 (40)10 (41)0 (42)6
(43)18 (44)10 (45)18 (46)2 (47)18 (48)10
(49)8 (50)12 (51)18 (52)4 (53)16 (54)8
(55)4 (56)12 (57)8 (58)0 (59)10 (60)18
Page 9, Item 1:
(1)14 (2)14 (3)8 (4)0 (5)4 (6)12 (7)4 (8)4
(9)16 (10)12 (11)10 (12)4 (13)14 (14)6
(15)0 (16)12 (17)4 (18)12 (19)6 (20)2
(21)12 (22)4 (23)12 (24)12 (25)6 (26)10
(27)18 (28)12 (29)0 (30)0 (31)6 (32)14
(33)4 (34)0 (35)12 (36)18 (37)0 (38)4 (39)0
(40)18 (41)6 (42)2 (43)8 (44)14 (45)0

(46)12 (47)12 (48)8 (49)4 (50)6 (51)2
(52)18 (53)8 (54)10 (55)14 (56)16 (57)16
(58)4 (59)4 (60)0
Page 10, Item 1:
(1)4 (2)2 (3)2 (4)18 (5)10 (6)8 (7)14 (8)18
(9)18 (10)0 (11)6 (12)0 (13)8 (14)2 (15)4
(16)4 (17)0 (18)0 (19)18 (20)8 (21)18
(22)16 (23)14 (24)0 (25)4 (26)14 (27)0
(28)2 (29)2 (30)6 (31)4 (32)10 (33)0 (34)14
(35)6 (36)0 (37)6 (38)4 (39)14 (40)2 (41)12
(42)8 (43)10 (44)8 (45)8 (46)12 (47)6 (48)6
(49)14 (50)2 (51)10 (52)16 (53)0 (54)18
(55)0 (56)4 (57)0 (58)10 (59)8 (60)8
Page 11, Item 1:
(1)6 (2)12 (3)4 (4)14 (5)14 (6)18 (7)6 (8)4
(9)12 (10)12 (11)6 (12)14 (13)0 (14)18
(15)14 (16)2 (17)0 (18)12 (19)8 (20)14
(21)14 (22)18 (23)14 (24)16 (25)6 (26)0
(27)10 (28)18 (29)10 (30)8 (31)2 (32)18
(33)2 (34)16 (35)14 (36)14 (37)8 (38)8
(39)6 (40)2 (41)14 (42)14 (43)4 (44)12
(45)8 (46)10 (47)16 (48)12 (49)4 (50)2
(51)10 (52)12 (53)18 (54)4 (55)10 (56)18
(57)2 (58)14 (59)8 (60)0
Page 12, Item 1:
(1)14 (2)2 (3)2 (4)2 (5)10 (6)14 (7)0 (8)10
(9)12 (10)8 (11)2 (12)12 (13)12 (14)4
(15)12 (16)16 (17)12 (18)18 (19)6 (20)18
(21)18 (22)8 (23)0 (24)6 (25)4 (26)14

(27)12 (28)18 (29)2 (30)6 (31)10 (32)12
(33)14 (34)4 (35)6 (36)10 (37)6 (38)8
(39)10 (40)8 (41)14 (42)16 (43)6 (44)10
(45)8 (46)4 (47)12 (48)6 (49)0 (50)2 (51)18
(52)2 (53)0 (54)0 (55)12 (56)4 (57)2 (58)4
(59)14 (60)0

Page 13, Item 1:
(1)0 (2)27 (3)21 (4)6 (5)18 (6)24 (7)18
(8)21 (9)15 (10)12 (11)12 (12)21 (13)0
(14)27 (15)12 (16)9 (17)18 (18)3 (19)21
(20)9 (21)15 (22)24 (23)18 (24)12 (25)27
(26)21 (27)12 (28)27 (29)9 (30)18 (31)12
(32)15 (33)0 (34)9 (35)9 (36)24 (37)24
(38)12 (39)27 (40)27 (41)15 (42)18 (43)24
(44)24 (45)6 (46)15 (47)18 (48)9 (49)0
(50)18 (51)15 (52)6 (53)21 (54)24 (55)9
(56)18 (57)21 (58)21 (59)15 (60)6
Page 14, Item 1:
(1)9 (2)15 (3)6 (4)9 (5)0 (6)18 (7)21 (8)15
(9)9 (10)24 (11)24 (12)18 (13)0 (14)24
(15)6 (16)12 (17)21 (18)24 (19)9 (20)18
(21)21 (22)15 (23)18 (24)18 (25)21 (26)9
(27)21 (28)18 (29)15 (30)24 (31)12 (32)15
(33)0 (34)18 (35)12 (36)21 (37)27 (38)0
(39)27 (40)24 (41)9 (42)12 (43)6 (44)6
(45)3 (46)24 (47)9 (48)24 (49)21 (50)24
(51)21 (52)12 (53)9 (54)9 (55)15 (56)12
(57)15 (58)0 (59)18 (60)0
Page 15, Item 1:
(1)18 (2)21 (3)12 (4)21 (5)18 (6)6 (7)24
(8)0 (9)21 (10)0 (11)24 (12)18 (13)9 (14)12
(15)21 (16)0 (17)21 (18)21 (19)12 (20)12
(21)0 (22)18 (23)15 (24)12 (25)0 (26)24
(27)27 (28)6 (29)18 (30)9 (31)27 (32)18
(33)18 (34)9 (35)9 (36)18 (37)3 (38)15
(39)0 (40)21 (41)27 (42)9 (43)9 (44)9 (45)0
(46)12 (47)24 (48)15 (49)18 (50)6 (51)24
(52)21 (53)18 (54)3 (55)15 (56)3 (57)15
(58)15 (59)12 (60)27
Page 16, Item 1:
(1)0 (2)24 (3)21 (4)24 (5)18 (6)24 (7)27
(8)27 (9)12 (10)0 (11)27 (12)9 (13)18
(14)15 (15)21 (16)21 (17)12 (18)27 (19)0
(20)15 (21)27 (22)3 (23)3 (24)21 (25)27
(26)0 (27)9 (28)6 (29)3 (30)0 (31)6 (32)12
(33)15 (34)18 (35)21 (36)24 (37)18 (38)9

(39)27 (40)3 (41)12 (42)6 (43)3 (44)15
(45)21 (46)9 (47)24 (48)24 (49)15 (50)15
(51)6 (52)6 (53)24 (54)6 (55)12 (56)27
(57)9 (58)0 (59)6 (60)15
Page 17, Item 1:
(1)6 (2)12 (3)9 (4)0 (5)21 (6)6 (7)6 (8)3 (9)9
(10)0 (11)12 (12)0 (13)21 (14)24 (15)27
(16)15 (17)15 (18)27 (19)24 (20)3 (21)0
(22)6 (23)18 (24)15 (25)12 (26)15 (27)0
(28)21 (29)6 (30)12 (31)18 (32)0 (33)6
(34)27 (35)24 (36)18 (37)21 (38)18 (39)18
(40)18 (41)15 (42)27 (43)27 (44)27 (45)0
(46)18 (47)6 (48)6 (49)15 (50)18 (51)27
(52)21 (53)3 (54)6 (55)12 (56)6 (57)21
(58)24 (59)6 (60)24
Page 18, Item 1:
(1)15 (2)15 (3)6 (4)3 (5)9 (6)12 (7)21 (8)24
(9)27 (10)24 (11)21 (12)9 (13)27 (14)6
(15)15 (16)21 (17)0 (18)18 (19)6 (20)21
(21)15 (22)6 (23)3 (24)12 (25)24 (26)18
(27)24 (28)15 (29)18 (30)15 (31)15 (32)0
(33)18 (34)15 (35)6 (36)12 (37)9 (38)3
(39)15 (40)12 (41)6 (42)0 (43)0 (44)6
(45)24 (46)9 (47)15 (48)9 (49)21 (50)12
(51)12 (52)12 (53)27 (54)12 (55)24 (56)9
(57)21 (58)3 (59)18 (60)18
Page 19, Item 1:
(1)24 (2)24 (3)0 (4)12 (5)24 (6)12 (7)24
(8)9 (9)27 (10)24 (11)9 (12)18 (13)21 (14)3

(15)9 (16)21 (17)12 (18)12 (19)18 (20)6
(21)6 (22)6 (23)15 (24)24 (25)0 (26)27
(27)18 (28)6 (29)15 (30)15 (31)6 (32)0
(33)6 (34)9 (35)6 (36)12 (37)27 (38)15
(39)3 (40)24 (41)21 (42)21 (43)3 (44)27
(45)15 (46)15 (47)9 (48)27 (49)0 (50)0
(51)15 (52)21 (53)27 (54)15 (55)21 (56)0
(57)15 (58)9 (59)18 (60)24

Page 22, Item 1:
(1)4 (2)8 (3)24 (4)16 (5)4 (6)8 (7)20 (8)24
(9)20 (10)24 (11)24 (12)20 (13)32 (14)32
(15)28 (16)36 (17)32 (18)0 (19)8 (20)8
(21)36 (22)0 (23)24 (24)36 (25)8 (26)16
(27)16 (28)4 (29)28 (30)24 (31)36 (32)20
(33)12 (34)12 (35)36 (36)12 (37)0 (38)24
(39)36 (40)20 (41)4 (42)4 (43)16 (44)0
(45)20 (46)24 (47)12 (48)4 (49)32 (50)12
(51)4 (52)24 (53)32 (54)36 (55)32 (56)36
(57)4 (58)24 (59)24 (60)4

Page 23, Item 1:
(1)32 (2)8 (3)24 (4)36 (5)36 (6)12 (7)32
(8)28 (9)28 (10)16 (11)12 (12)16 (13)36
(14)8 (15)4 (16)4 (17)4 (18)24 (19)8 (20)16
(21)32 (22)12 (23)32 (24)4 (25)4 (26)8
(27)32 (28)16 (29)0 (30)4 (31)28 (32)20
(33)24 (34)0 (35)0 (36)24 (37)16 (38)12
(39)36 (40)32 (41)32 (42)28 (43)20 (44)36
(45)28 (46)4 (47)4 (48)4 (49)28 (50)20
(51)0 (52)32 (53)36 (54)16 (55)8 (56)0
(57)12 (58)0 (59)20 (60)36

Page 24, Item 1:
(1)28 (2)12 (3)8 (4)32 (5)28 (6)28 (7)0
(8)12 (9)4 (10)16 (11)32 (12)32 (13)16
(14)8 (15)32 (16)32 (17)20 (18)16 (19)4
(20)24 (21)20 (22)32 (23)16 (24)0 (25)24
(26)20 (27)4 (28)32 (29)16 (30)8 (31)4
(32)4 (33)20 (34)16 (35)32 (36)20 (37)4
(38)0 (39)28 (40)24 (41)12 (42)16 (43)12
(44)0 (45)16 (46)20 (47)12 (48)0 (49)16
(50)28 (51)28 (52)28 (53)20 (54)32 (55)16
(56)16 (57)32 (58)20 (59)28 (60)8

Page 25, Item 1:
(1)20 (2)8 (3)36 (4)8 (5)4 (6)28 (7)16 (8)12
(9)16 (10)24 (11)32 (12)36 (13)8 (14)16
(15)32 (16)24 (17)24 (18)20 (19)36 (20)28
(21)12 (22)32 (23)24 (24)4 (25)20 (26)0
(27)0 (28)0 (29)32 (30)28 (31)16 (32)32
(33)24 (34)0 (35)12 (36)8 (37)16 (38)4

(39)8 (40)36 (41)20 (42)24 (43)20 (44)36
(45)32 (46)28 (47)12 (48)36 (49)12 (50)4
(51)24 (52)16 (53)4 (54)32 (55)20 (56)20
(57)0 (58)16 (59)12 (60)4

Page 26, Item 1:
(1)4 (2)0 (3)20 (4)32 (5)36 (6)24 (7)8 (8)4
(9)8 (10)16 (11)28 (12)32 (13)12 (14)24
(15)8 (16)4 (17)20 (18)36 (19)12 (20)28
(21)0 (22)0 (23)24 (24)16 (25)0 (26)36
(27)28 (28)8 (29)16 (30)28 (31)32 (32)16
(33)36 (34)0 (35)36 (36)12 (37)20 (38)24
(39)8 (40)28 (41)16 (42)32 (43)28 (44)4
(45)28 (46)12 (47)12 (48)16 (49)4 (50)24
(51)24 (52)16 (53)0 (54)24 (55)0 (56)36
(57)36 (58)12 (59)32 (60)16

Page 27, Item 1:
(1)12 (2)0 (3)12 (4)36 (5)24 (6)24 (7)12
(8)20 (9)36 (10)28 (11)20 (12)12 (13)8
(14)8 (15)0 (16)16 (17)20 (18)32 (19)0
(20)0 (21)0 (22)20 (23)16 (24)20 (25)36
(26)20 (27)8 (28)8 (29)8 (30)20 (31)16
(32)20 (33)4 (34)8 (35)0 (36)36 (37)8 (38)0
(39)24 (40)8 (41)20 (42)8 (43)12 (44)24
(45)0 (46)36 (47)16 (48)20 (49)12 (50)16
(51)8 (52)28 (53)12 (54)16 (55)20 (56)0
(57)24 (58)4 (59)16 (60)12

Page 28, Item 1:
(1)20 (2)8 (3)36 (4)8 (5)4 (6)16 (7)8 (8)32
(9)36 (10)32 (11)4 (12)8 (13)12 (14)36

(15)28 (16)32 (17)8 (18)8 (19)20 (20)28
(21)0 (22)36 (23)28 (24)24 (25)16 (26)28
(27)32 (28)28 (29)36 (30)24 (31)16 (32)24
(33)32 (34)28 (35)28 (36)20 (37)0 (38)16
(39)4 (40)24 (41)36 (42)0 (43)32 (44)36
(45)0 (46)12 (47)32 (48)4 (49)28 (50)16
(51)24 (52)4 (53)28 (54)36 (55)8 (56)4
(57)4 (58)36 (59)24 (60)24

Page 31, Item 1:
(1)5 (2)0 (3)20 (4)35 (5)20 (6)45 (7)35 (8)0
(9)15 (10)45 (11)35 (12)15 (13)20 (14)35
(15)40 (16)15 (17)25 (18)45 (19)45 (20)35
(21)10 (22)20 (23)5 (24)20 (25)10 (26)30
(27)0 (28)5 (29)20 (30)30 (31)0 (32)0 (33)5
(34)40 (35)0 (36)20 (37)40 (38)45 (39)0
(40)0 (41)45 (42)0 (43)20 (44)30 (45)25
(46)10 (47)10 (48)40 (49)45 (50)10 (51)0
(52)25 (53)40 (54)5 (55)45 (56)35 (57)25
(58)25 (59)15 (60)20
Page 32, Item 1:
(1)45 (2)40 (3)40 (4)5 (5)5 (6)15 (7)30
(8)20 (9)0 (10)40 (11)30 (12)15 (13)35
(14)20 (15)30 (16)35 (17)25 (18)25 (19)10
(20)45 (21)30 (22)20 (23)25 (24)35 (25)0
(26)0 (27)15 (28)10 (29)40 (30)30 (31)30
(32)25 (33)5 (34)15 (35)40 (36)25 (37)40
(38)40 (39)45 (40)5 (41)35 (42)25 (43)30
(44)25 (45)35 (46)45 (47)0 (48)40 (49)5
(50)30 (51)40 (52)40 (53)5 (54)35 (55)5
(56)45 (57)30 (58)45 (59)25 (60)20
Page 33, Item 1:
(1)20 (2)30 (3)30 (4)10 (5)15 (6)30 (7)20
(8)15 (9)25 (10)5 (11)20 (12)35 (13)40
(14)0 (15)40 (16)30 (17)35 (18)40 (19)20
(20)0 (21)0 (22)45 (23)5 (24)35 (25)35
(26)30 (27)30 (28)30 (29)40 (30)45 (31)25
(32)5 (33)20 (34)40 (35)20 (36)35 (37)25
(38)10 (39)40 (40)0 (41)15 (42)15 (43)40
(44)0 (45)45 (46)30 (47)0 (48)15 (49)0
(50)15 (51)25 (52)5 (53)10 (54)25 (55)30
(56)35 (57)20 (58)0 (59)5 (60)5
Page 34, Item 1:
(1)5 (2)10 (3)10 (4)15 (5)25 (6)35 (7)35
(8)25 (9)30 (10)15 (11)20 (12)15 (13)15
(14)5 (15)30 (16)5 (17)45 (18)20 (19)25
(20)20 (21)5 (22)30 (23)45 (24)0 (25)25
(26)30 (27)0 (28)0 (29)5 (30)45 (31)25
(32)45 (33)5 (34)5 (35)0 (36)15 (37)0

(38)45 (39)15 (40)25 (41)45 (42)35 (43)5
(44)45 (45)20 (46)30 (47)30 (48)25 (49)30
(50)20 (51)30 (52)0 (53)45 (54)10 (55)0
(56)40 (57)0 (58)25 (59)35 (60)5
Page 35, Item 1:
(1)20 (2)45 (3)10 (4)5 (5)45 (6)20 (7)45
(8)30 (9)0 (10)5 (11)20 (12)5 (13)35 (14)15
(15)15 (16)15 (17)5 (18)25 (19)25 (20)10
(21)20 (22)40 (23)40 (24)30 (25)10 (26)5
(27)40 (28)40 (29)20 (30)35 (31)20 (32)35
(33)0 (34)5 (35)20 (36)5 (37)30 (38)25
(39)40 (40)30 (41)45 (42)20 (43)15 (44)20
(45)20 (46)20 (47)45 (48)0 (49)45 (50)20
(51)15 (52)10 (53)45 (54)0 (55)10 (56)25
(57)0 (58)25 (59)10 (60)40
Page 36, Item 1:
(1)35 (2)5 (3)15 (4)45 (5)25 (6)5 (7)5 (8)45
(9)0 (10)35 (11)45 (12)15 (13)30 (14)20
(15)10 (16)0 (17)10 (18)15 (19)25 (20)45
(21)35 (22)5 (23)25 (24)15 (25)20 (26)15
(27)35 (28)35 (29)45 (30)45 (31)40 (32)45
(33)40 (34)30 (35)30 (36)5 (37)35 (38)35
(39)20 (40)40 (41)30 (42)0 (43)40 (44)25
(45)45 (46)5 (47)5 (48)0 (49)10 (50)35
(51)10 (52)25 (53)35 (54)35 (55)0 (56)25
(57)15 (58)0 (59)40 (60)25
Page 37, Item 1:
(1)0 (2)15 (3)30 (4)30 (5)0 (6)0 (7)0 (8)30
(9)35 (10)45 (11)15 (12)30 (13)20 (14)45

(15)20 (16)5 (17)5 (18)15 (19)45 (20)40
(21)15 (22)30 (23)10 (24)15 (25)0 (26)40
(27)40 (28)35 (29)20 (30)20 (31)35 (32)35
(33)0 (34)35 (35)0 (36)30 (37)45 (38)10
(39)5 (40)30 (41)35 (42)25 (43)35 (44)0
(45)20 (46)15 (47)5 (48)5 (49)15 (50)0
(51)5 (52)10 (53)10 (54)35 (55)5 (56)0
(57)25 (58)0 (59)20 (60)40

Page 40, Item 1:
(1)24 (2)30 (3)30 (4)48 (5)48 (6)6 (7)6 (8)6
(9)36 (10)0 (11)18 (12)6 (13)0 (14)0 (15)0
(16)0 (17)12 (18)42 (19)0 (20)24 (21)12
(22)24 (23)12 (24)42 (25)30 (26)6 (27)0
(28)12 (29)0 (30)36 (31)36 (32)30 (33)6
(34)12 (35)6 (36)6 (37)30 (38)48 (39)30
(40)42 (41)18 (42)48 (43)42 (44)12 (45)18
(46)24 (47)24 (48)36 (49)24 (50)0 (51)36
(52)30 (53)30 (54)54 (55)36 (56)54 (57)0
(58)12 (59)24 (60)24
Page 41, Item 1:
(1)0 (2)12 (3)42 (4)54 (5)6 (6)24 (7)24
(8)42 (9)24 (10)6 (11)24 (12)54 (13)24
(14)6 (15)24 (16)6 (17)12 (18)54 (19)18
(20)24 (21)30 (22)6 (23)54 (24)24 (25)0
(26)6 (27)18 (28)54 (29)36 (30)0 (31)18
(32)0 (33)48 (34)30 (35)30 (36)48 (37)12
(38)36 (39)36 (40)6 (41)48 (42)6 (43)24
(44)12 (45)54 (46)36 (47)0 (48)42 (49)30
(50)0 (51)42 (52)12 (53)48 (54)42 (55)54
(56)0 (57)12 (58)36 (59)42 (60)24
Page 42, Item 1:
(1)12 (2)30 (3)18 (4)54 (5)48 (6)48 (7)54
(8)48 (9)54 (10)24 (11)0 (12)6 (13)18
(14)30 (15)18 (16)6 (17)24 (18)12 (19)24
(20)24 (21)42 (22)30 (23)36 (24)42 (25)30
(26)30 (27)12 (28)30 (29)54 (30)36 (31)42
(32)36 (33)48 (34)30 (35)48 (36)42 (37)36
(38)30 (39)42 (40)12 (41)12 (42)18 (43)42
(44)48 (45)36 (46)18 (47)24 (48)48 (49)0
(50)12 (51)12 (52)30 (53)30 (54)0 (55)24
(56)18 (57)6 (58)6 (59)42 (60)54
Page 43, Item 1:
(1)42 (2)48 (3)12 (4)36 (5)6 (6)24 (7)30
(8)6 (9)6 (10)30 (11)36 (12)42 (13)24 (14)0
(15)30 (16)12 (17)24 (18)30 (19)12 (20)12
(21)24 (22)6 (23)6 (24)0 (25)0 (26)24
(27)24 (28)24 (29)24 (30)30 (31)36 (32)24
(33)54 (34)36 (35)0 (36)24 (37)18 (38)18

(39)18 (40)12 (41)0 (42)42 (43)42 (44)54
(45)12 (46)42 (47)42 (48)6 (49)36 (50)18
(51)42 (52)42 (53)18 (54)54 (55)30 (56)24
(57)24 (58)30 (59)6 (60)30
Page 44, Item 1:
(1)12 (2)36 (3)48 (4)36 (5)42 (6)18 (7)24
(8)54 (9)0 (10)0 (11)36 (12)54 (13)30
(14)30 (15)18 (16)42 (17)54 (18)36 (19)6
(20)54 (21)42 (22)30 (23)24 (24)36 (25)24
(26)0 (27)48 (28)36 (29)18 (30)42 (31)0
(32)36 (33)18 (34)36 (35)48 (36)36 (37)0
(38)18 (39)30 (40)54 (41)36 (42)54 (43)12
(44)18 (45)54 (46)24 (47)54 (48)42 (49)6
(50)36 (51)6 (52)54 (53)48 (54)36 (55)54
(56)0 (57)42 (58)54 (59)24 (60)30
Page 45, Item 1:
(1)0 (2)12 (3)42 (4)12 (5)12 (6)36 (7)48
(8)24 (9)30 (10)30 (11)42 (12)6 (13)30
(14)36 (15)48 (16)36 (17)12 (18)12 (19)12
(20)36 (21)42 (22)36 (23)48 (24)36 (25)42
(26)36 (27)18 (28)18 (29)24 (30)42 (31)48
(32)6 (33)18 (34)48 (35)18 (36)48 (37)42
(38)30 (39)12 (40)42 (41)0 (42)24 (43)0
(44)48 (45)24 (46)54 (47)48 (48)0 (49)42
(50)0 (51)6 (52)6 (53)30 (54)48 (55)54
(56)6 (57)48 (58)6 (59)36 (60)30
Page 46, Item 1:
(1)0 (2)6 (3)36 (4)48 (5)54 (6)18 (7)18
(8)12 (9)48 (10)30 (11)36 (12)12 (13)18

(14)6 (15)0 (16)48 (17)6 (18)54 (19)54
(20)42 (21)18 (22)48 (23)42 (24)42 (25)36
(26)36 (27)30 (28)48 (29)0 (30)54 (31)12
(32)30 (33)54 (34)6 (35)30 (36)42 (37)6
(38)54 (39)48 (40)0 (41)36 (42)36 (43)42
(44)30 (45)36 (46)36 (47)48 (48)54 (49)42
(50)6 (51)36 (52)18 (53)0 (54)18 (55)36
(56)24 (57)12 (58)48 (59)48 (60)0

Page 49, Item 1:

(1)56 (2)7 (3)21 (4)21 (5)56 (6)56 (7)35
(8)49 (9)28 (10)56 (11)49 (12)14 (13)14
(14)21 (15)21 (16)28 (17)56 (18)49 (19)7
(20)28 (21)56 (22)28 (23)42 (24)28 (25)0
(26)63 (27)63 (28)14 (29)7 (30)21 (31)28
(32)63 (33)49 (34)14 (35)21 (36)21 (37)42
(38)21 (39)42 (40)21 (41)14 (42)21 (43)7
(44)56 (45)49 (46)7 (47)63 (48)14 (49)56
(50)49 (51)56 (52)0 (53)7 (54)7 (55)21
(56)63 (57)28 (58)0 (59)35 (60)42

Page 50, Item 1:

(1)21 (2)21 (3)21 (4)49 (5)21 (6)42 (7)7
(8)49 (9)35 (10)28 (11)21 (12)35 (13)63
(14)49 (15)56 (16)56 (17)21 (18)56 (19)28
(20)56 (21)35 (22)56 (23)63 (24)21 (25)63
(26)63 (27)56 (28)21 (29)56 (30)56 (31)49
(32)7 (33)0 (34)49 (35)35 (36)7 (37)63
(38)14 (39)56 (40)0 (41)56 (42)28 (43)7
(44)21 (45)35 (46)63 (47)49 (48)42 (49)42
(50)56 (51)14 (52)56 (53)0 (54)63 (55)21
(56)0 (57)21 (58)49 (59)0 (60)49

Page 51, Item 1:

(1)49 (2)56 (3)21 (4)7 (5)56 (6)49 (7)35
(8)63 (9)63 (10)35 (11)63 (12)42 (13)0
(14)49 (15)42 (16)28 (17)35 (18)28 (19)7
(20)35 (21)0 (22)56 (23)7 (24)35 (25)42
(26)14 (27)14 (28)42 (29)63 (30)35 (31)14
(32)56 (33)35 (34)7 (35)35 (36)7 (37)35
(38)42 (39)21 (40)63 (41)63 (42)49 (43)35
(44)0 (45)7 (46)49 (47)35 (48)63 (49)0
(50)21 (51)56 (52)0 (53)35 (54)49 (55)14
(56)0 (57)28 (58)56 (59)21 (60)0

Page 52, Item 1:

(1)21 (2)56 (3)49 (4)49 (5)49 (6)35 (7)42
(8)49 (9)21 (10)21 (11)63 (12)0 (13)0
(14)21 (15)21 (16)49 (17)42 (18)63 (19)35
(20)14 (21)42 (22)63 (23)0 (24)35 (25)56
(26)63 (27)14 (28)63 (29)63 (30)0 (31)49
(32)63 (33)7 (34)63 (35)35 (36)49 (37)42
(38)49 (39)14 (40)14 (41)14 (42)28 (43)14
(44)7 (45)35 (46)49 (47)0 (48)0 (49)49
(50)7 (51)14 (52)63 (53)63 (54)35 (55)14
(56)21 (57)63 (58)7 (59)21 (60)28

Page 53, Item 1:

(1)0 (2)42 (3)35 (4)63 (5)63 (6)42 (7)0
(8)35 (9)21 (10)14 (11)35 (12)28 (13)35
(14)56 (15)42 (16)42 (17)0 (18)14 (19)56
(20)28 (21)56 (22)63 (23)0 (24)14 (25)49
(26)0 (27)21 (28)56 (29)56 (30)35 (31)0
(32)49 (33)28 (34)35 (35)14 (36)49 (37)21
(38)49 (39)0 (40)35 (41)7 (42)14 (43)14
(44)7 (45)56 (46)14 (47)35 (48)63 (49)0
(50)56 (51)35 (52)14 (53)0 (54)14 (55)42
(56)49 (57)42 (58)42 (59)21 (60)42

Page 54, Item 1:

(1)42 (2)35 (3)0 (4)14 (5)35 (6)42 (7)56
(8)49 (9)56 (10)0 (11)35 (12)21 (13)14
(14)28 (15)28 (16)42 (17)35 (18)21 (19)21
(20)63 (21)14 (22)28 (23)56 (24)28 (25)56
(26)14 (27)42 (28)0 (29)49 (30)7 (31)42
(32)49 (33)63 (34)21 (35)21 (36)21 (37)63
(38)0 (39)49 (40)63 (41)42 (42)63 (43)21
(44)28 (45)28 (46)49 (47)21 (48)21 (49)42
(50)35 (51)35 (52)7 (53)0 (54)14 (55)14
(56)0 (57)21 (58)42 (59)63 (60)49

Page 55, Item 1:

(1)35 (2)35 (3)63 (4)0 (5)28 (6)7 (7)28
(8)35 (9)49 (10)21 (11)28 (12)7 (13)14

(14)49 (15)63 (16)63 (17)56 (18)42 (19)28
(20)63 (21)35 (22)0 (23)14 (24)49 (25)63
(26)56 (27)21 (28)35 (29)21 (30)56 (31)63
(32)42 (33)0 (34)21 (35)21 (36)0 (37)56
(38)35 (39)0 (40)28 (41)14 (42)7 (43)7
(44)49 (45)21 (46)49 (47)35 (48)21 (49)56
(50)35 (51)28 (52)35 (53)35 (54)35 (55)42
(56)0 (57)63 (58)63 (59)0 (60)63

Page 48, Item 1:
(1)32 (2)24 (3)48 (4)24 (5)24 (6)8 (7)64
(8)0 (9)24 (10)48 (11)48 (12)40 (13)40
(14)16 (15)40 (16)16 (17)0 (18)8 (19)56
(20)56 (21)72 (22)64 (23)8 (24)48 (25)0
(26)40 (27)24 (28)8 (29)24 (30)48 (31)8
(32)24 (33)32 (34)40 (35)72 (36)0 (37)56
(38)64 (39)40 (40)0 (41)40 (42)0 (43)24
(44)24 (45)16 (46)32 (47)24 (48)56 (49)16
(50)0 (51)24 (52)48 (53)48 (54)24 (55)16
(56)32 (57)32 (58)40 (59)40 (60)48
Page 49, Item 1:
(1)8 (2)64 (3)40 (4)32 (5)8 (6)24 (7)8 (8)40
(9)40 (10)16 (11)56 (12)72 (13)40 (14)16
(15)40 (16)72 (17)24 (18)8 (19)16 (20)32
(21)56 (22)48 (23)16 (24)32 (25)16 (26)64
(27)40 (28)16 (29)72 (30)72 (31)72 (32)8
(33)16 (34)40 (35)32 (36)0 (37)0 (38)40
(39)64 (40)16 (41)32 (42)64 (43)64 (44)24
(45)72 (46)56 (47)8 (48)0 (49)64 (50)72
(51)32 (52)64 (53)32 (54)32 (55)40 (56)64
(57)72 (58)56 (59)16 (60)32
Page 50, Item 1:
(1)32 (2)8 (3)48 (4)24 (5)24 (6)24 (7)64
(8)72 (9)16 (10)72 (11)40 (12)8 (13)56
(14)40 (15)40 (16)64 (17)24 (18)40 (19)56
(20)8 (21)64 (22)32 (23)48 (24)16 (25)40
(26)72 (27)40 (28)40 (29)48 (30)8 (31)56
(32)48 (33)16 (34)0 (35)16 (36)16 (37)0
(38)16 (39)16 (40)8 (41)8 (42)8 (43)32
(44)56 (45)0 (46)32 (47)8 (48)56 (49)24
(50)40 (51)24 (52)16 (53)72 (54)0 (55)72
(56)72 (57)40 (58)72 (59)24 (60)40
Page 51, Item 1:
(1)48 (2)24 (3)48 (4)32 (5)24 (6)32 (7)64
(8)40 (9)64 (10)0 (11)64 (12)16 (13)0
(14)40 (15)72 (16)8 (17)56 (18)8 (19)0
(20)32 (21)56 (22)64 (23)72 (24)64 (25)48
(26)56 (27)8 (28)40 (29)16 (30)16 (31)8
(32)32 (33)72 (34)72 (35)24 (36)0 (37)40
(38)8 (39)72 (40)64 (41)16 (42)48 (43)16
(44)8 (45)8 (46)0 (47)40 (48)24 (49)56
(50)72 (51)24 (52)0 (53)16 (54)64 (55)48
(56)40 (57)48 (58)48 (59)24 (60)56
Page 52, Item 1:
(1)32 (2)16 (3)32 (4)56 (5)24 (6)56 (7)8
(8)16 (9)72 (10)8 (11)0 (12)24 (13)16 (14)8
(15)0 (16)8 (17)16 (18)72 (19)32 (20)32
(21)24 (22)8 (23)32 (24)72 (25)72 (26)8
(27)8 (28)48 (29)48 (30)72 (31)64 (32)0
(33)48 (34)48 (35)40 (36)56 (37)72 (38)48
(39)48 (40)48 (41)64 (42)0 (43)72 (44)56
(45)0 (46)0 (47)16 (48)56 (49)8 (50)0
(51)16 (52)56 (53)40 (54)32 (55)48 (56)24
(57)24 (58)32 (59)32 (60)56
Page 53, Item 1:
(1)40 (2)72 (3)8 (4)72 (5)16 (6)64 (7)40
(8)48 (9)8 (10)72 (11)64 (12)48 (13)40
(14)72 (15)72 (16)56 (17)0 (18)72 (19)48
(20)56 (21)40 (22)56 (23)48 (24)32 (25)0
(26)8 (27)24 (28)64 (29)72 (30)40 (31)64
(32)32 (33)16 (34)56 (35)64 (36)40 (37)56
(38)56 (39)48 (40)72 (41)64 (42)72 (43)64
(44)56 (45)24 (46)40 (47)48 (48)0 (49)40
(50)24 (51)8 (52)72 (53)64 (54)8 (55)64
(56)8 (57)32 (58)8 (59)40 (60)16
Page 54, Item 1:
(1)0 (2)56 (3)16 (4)24 (5)40 (6)48 (7)32
(8)0 (9)40 (10)48 (11)40 (12)72 (13)40

(14)0 (15)16 (16)40 (17)48 (18)16 (19)56
(20)48 (21)0 (22)48 (23)8 (24)48 (25)56
(26)64 (27)72 (28)56 (29)40 (30)72 (31)72
(32)56 (33)64 (34)32 (35)24 (36)72 (37)48
(38)24 (39)56 (40)56 (41)72 (42)32 (43)48
(44)40 (45)72 (46)72 (47)32 (48)40 (49)8
(50)16 (51)24 (52)8 (53)0 (54)16 (55)48
(56)72 (57)64 (58)48 (59)16 (60)72

Page 55, Item 1:

(1)81 (2)36 (3)72 (4)18 (5)54 (6)18 (7)81
(8)36 (9)9 (10)81 (11)54 (12)0 (13)63
(14)18 (15)63 (16)27 (17)63 (18)63 (19)27
(20)36 (21)9 (22)45 (23)27 (24)36 (25)81
(26)63 (27)81 (28)81 (29)36 (30)72 (31)81
(32)63 (33)27 (34)9 (35)0 (36)72 (37)27
(38)81 (39)72 (40)9 (41)63 (42)36 (43)9
(44)63 (45)81 (46)0 (47)45 (48)72 (49)0
(50)45 (51)36 (52)36 (53)0 (54)27 (55)27
(56)27 (57)36 (58)18 (59)45 (60)63

Page 56, Item 1:

(1)0 (2)54 (3)81 (4)45 (5)45 (6)18 (7)54
(8)45 (9)27 (10)72 (11)54 (12)81 (13)72
(14)36 (15)0 (16)27 (17)36 (18)72 (19)45
(20)18 (21)0 (22)72 (23)27 (24)0 (25)0
(26)72 (27)18 (28)72 (29)0 (30)18 (31)63
(32)72 (33)0 (34)0 (35)45 (36)72 (37)72
(38)18 (39)36 (40)36 (41)63 (42)54 (43)36
(44)54 (45)45 (46)54 (47)27 (48)63 (49)0
(50)54 (51)27 (52)63 (53)36 (54)0 (55)63
(56)36 (57)72 (58)0 (59)18 (60)36

Page 57, Item 1:

(1)36 (2)72 (3)27 (4)9 (5)81 (6)0 (7)0 (8)45
(9)72 (10)9 (11)72 (12)36 (13)36 (14)72
(15)81 (16)27 (17)72 (18)45 (19)9 (20)9
(21)45 (22)9 (23)63 (24)0 (25)27 (26)45
(27)54 (28)27 (29)54 (30)45 (31)45 (32)0
(33)27 (34)72 (35)54 (36)63 (37)72 (38)45
(39)45 (40)54 (41)0 (42)9 (43)27 (44)27
(45)72 (46)72 (47)45 (48)81 (49)54 (50)0
(51)0 (52)27 (53)72 (54)54 (55)9 (56)72
(57)27 (58)63 (59)18 (60)81

Page 58, Item 1:

(1)63 (2)27 (3)54 (4)81 (5)18 (6)72 (7)27
(8)9 (9)81 (10)72 (11)54 (12)9 (13)0 (14)63
(15)81 (16)36 (17)9 (18)63 (19)72 (20)72
(21)27 (22)45 (23)0 (24)0 (25)18 (26)45
(27)0 (28)9 (29)18 (30)36 (31)18 (32)63
(33)36 (34)18 (35)81 (36)54 (37)9 (38)54

(39)36 (40)45 (41)72 (42)9 (43)18 (44)27
(45)72 (46)36 (47)9 (48)0 (49)63 (50)54
(51)36 (52)72 (53)63 (54)54 (55)36 (56)36
(57)36 (58)27 (59)54 (60)81

Page 59, Item 1:

(1)18 (2)81 (3)36 (4)9 (5)54 (6)0 (7)36
(8)27 (9)45 (10)27 (11)63 (12)63 (13)9
(14)18 (15)63 (16)18 (17)63 (18)0 (19)63
(20)81 (21)81 (22)45 (23)0 (24)63 (25)9
(26)18 (27)45 (28)45 (29)72 (30)45 (31)45
(32)27 (33)36 (34)81 (35)81 (36)18 (37)27
(38)72 (39)72 (40)45 (41)63 (42)0 (43)36
(44)9 (45)9 (46)18 (47)27 (48)36 (49)72
(50)63 (51)54 (52)27 (53)63 (54)27 (55)54
(56)9 (57)72 (58)27 (59)72 (60)18

Page 60, Item 1:

(1)45 (2)81 (3)81 (4)72 (5)27 (6)0 (7)18
(8)54 (9)81 (10)27 (11)72 (12)27 (13)72
(14)9 (15)27 (16)9 (17)81 (18)9 (19)0
(20)27 (21)0 (22)63 (23)72 (24)18 (25)54
(26)45 (27)36 (28)36 (29)45 (30)72 (31)36
(32)63 (33)54 (34)9 (35)36 (36)36 (37)63
(38)9 (39)54 (40)72 (41)54 (42)45 (43)36
(44)0 (45)45 (46)36 (47)27 (48)36 (49)81
(50)54 (51)27 (52)54 (53)63 (54)72 (55)81
(56)45 (57)0 (58)72 (59)18 (60)0

Page 61, Item 1:

(1)72 (2)63 (3)36 (4)81 (5)45 (6)36 (7)63
(8)63 (9)45 (10)0 (11)63 (12)27 (13)27

(14)81 (15)81 (16)9 (17)63 (18)36 (19)72
(20)54 (21)27 (22)63 (23)54 (24)81 (25)45
(26)45 (27)18 (28)45 (29)72 (30)72 (31)18
(32)0 (33)72 (34)27 (35)27 (36)36 (37)54
(38)0 (39)27 (40)54 (41)81 (42)27 (43)36
(44)63 (45)45 (46)36 (47)27 (48)63 (49)72
(50)18 (51)63 (52)72 (53)81 (54)72 (55)27
(56)45 (57)72 (58)72 (59)54 (60)81

Page 62, Item 1:

(1)60 (2)90 (3)60 (4)70 (5)70 (6)30 (7)80
(8)0 (9)10 (10)0 (11)0 (12)10 (13)10 (14)90
(15)70 (16)90 (17)40 (18)0 (19)0 (20)80
(21)30 (22)10 (23)70 (24)80 (25)70 (26)80
(27)0 (28)70 (29)0 (30)50 (31)60 (32)30
(33)0 (34)50 (35)40 (36)50 (37)40 (38)10
(39)50 (40)70 (41)80 (42)90 (43)30 (44)90
(45)90 (46)0 (47)40 (48)60 (49)60 (50)70
(51)70 (52)10 (53)30 (54)50 (55)60 (56)90
(57)0 (58)90 (59)30 (60)30

Page 63, Item 1:

(1)90 (2)20 (3)0 (4)90 (5)40 (6)60 (7)60
(8)30 (9)80 (10)10 (11)50 (12)50 (13)60
(14)10 (15)60 (16)60 (17)0 (18)10 (19)90
(20)50 (21)80 (22)50 (23)70 (24)50 (25)50
(26)40 (27)50 (28)0 (29)50 (30)90 (31)20
(32)60 (33)0 (34)10 (35)40 (36)30 (37)70
(38)40 (39)20 (40)0 (41)20 (42)20 (43)20
(44)0 (45)30 (46)0 (47)30 (48)40 (49)50
(50)80 (51)60 (52)0 (53)0 (54)50 (55)60
(56)30 (57)80 (58)70 (59)60 (60)30

Page 64, Item 1:

(1)90 (2)90 (3)0 (4)20 (5)40 (6)90 (7)20
(8)50 (9)0 (10)60 (11)40 (12)10 (13)70
(14)50 (15)50 (16)90 (17)40 (18)20 (19)30
(20)0 (21)30 (22)90 (23)30 (24)10 (25)40
(26)20 (27)20 (28)50 (29)10 (30)20 (31)20
(32)90 (33)90 (34)50 (35)0 (36)20 (37)10
(38)30 (39)60 (40)20 (41)80 (42)0 (43)70
(44)10 (45)60 (46)20 (47)30 (48)40 (49)60
(50)30 (51)0 (52)80 (53)20 (54)20 (55)10
(56)70 (57)60 (58)50 (59)10 (60)60

Page 65, Item 1:

(1)20 (2)80 (3)10 (4)60 (5)50 (6)30 (7)50
(8)20 (9)60 (10)60 (11)60 (12)90 (13)50
(14)0 (15)90 (16)90 (17)30 (18)0 (19)90
(20)10 (21)50 (22)10 (23)70 (24)80 (25)30
(26)90 (27)70 (28)60 (29)60 (30)0 (31)60
(32)40 (33)70 (34)40 (35)70 (36)0 (37)30

(38)40 (39)60 (40)60 (41)30 (42)50 (43)80
(44)50 (45)80 (46)40 (47)80 (48)60 (49)0
(50)40 (51)90 (52)40 (53)80 (54)70 (55)40
(56)0 (57)0 (58)20 (59)50 (60)40

Page 66, Item 1:

(1)90 (2)70 (3)80 (4)80 (5)30 (6)80 (7)60
(8)0 (9)60 (10)10 (11)20 (12)0 (13)60
(14)10 (15)60 (16)70 (17)10 (18)50 (19)70
(20)0 (21)10 (22)40 (23)30 (24)50 (25)10
(26)80 (27)0 (28)50 (29)60 (30)30 (31)20
(32)50 (33)90 (34)90 (35)80 (36)70 (37)10
(38)50 (39)60 (40)90 (41)70 (42)30 (43)30
(44)50 (45)80 (46)0 (47)60 (48)60 (49)60
(50)20 (51)10 (52)20 (53)90 (54)80 (55)20
(56)50 (57)90 (58)70 (59)30 (60)20

Page 67, Item 1:

(1)80 (2)0 (3)80 (4)20 (5)90 (6)40 (7)40
(8)80 (9)20 (10)20 (11)60 (12)90 (13)10
(14)60 (15)20 (16)10 (17)60 (18)70 (19)80
(20)0 (21)30 (22)30 (23)30 (24)80 (25)90
(26)30 (27)60 (28)60 (29)90 (30)80 (31)0
(32)30 (33)20 (34)10 (35)80 (36)80 (37)10
(38)90 (39)60 (40)30 (41)90 (42)60 (43)60
(44)10 (45)20 (46)30 (47)90 (48)10 (49)90
(50)0 (51)70 (52)0 (53)50 (54)70 (55)10
(56)10 (57)20 (58)80 (59)80 (60)10

Page 68, Item 1:

(1)40 (2)90 (3)60 (4)60 (5)10 (6)60 (7)90
(8)80 (9)90 (10)10 (11)60 (12)30 (13)80

(14)30 (15)40 (16)90 (17)60 (18)0 (19)50
(20)50 (21)30 (22)0 (23)60 (24)80 (25)70
(26)60 (27)50 (28)60 (29)40 (30)50 (31)90
(32)20 (33)60 (34)20 (35)50 (36)50 (37)30
(38)90 (39)80 (40)60 (41)80 (42)40 (43)20
(44)0 (45)20 (46)80 (47)30 (48)60 (49)30
(50)30 (51)60 (52)30 (53)20 (54)80 (55)0
(56)90 (57)70 (58)0 (59)0 (60)90

Page 69, Item 1:
(1)99 (2)33 (3)11 (4)33 (5)77 (6)11 (7)77
(8)11 (9)33 (10)77 (11)22 (12)55 (13)77
(14)55 (15)33 (16)0 (17)44 (18)55 (19)99
(20)44 (21)44 (22)0 (23)33 (24)0 (25)0
(26)77 (27)11 (28)0 (29)22 (30)0 (31)55
(32)55 (33)77 (34)0 (35)22 (36)55 (37)11
(38)33 (39)0 (40)66 (41)44 (42)33 (43)99
(44)22 (45)22 (46)11 (47)0 (48)88 (49)77
(50)55 (51)11 (52)11 (53)44 (54)77 (55)11
(56)77 (57)22 (58)66 (59)99 (60)88
Page 70, Item 1:
(1)77 (2)66 (3)77 (4)44 (5)88 (6)99 (7)77
(8)88 (9)22 (10)0 (11)33 (12)66 (13)22
(14)77 (15)44 (16)0 (17)99 (18)44 (19)99
(20)22 (21)55 (22)77 (23)0 (24)66 (25)0
(26)99 (27)0 (28)88 (29)99 (30)33 (31)0
(32)99 (33)0 (34)66 (35)99 (36)22 (37)77
(38)55 (39)0 (40)44 (41)55 (42)22 (43)88
(44)77 (45)77 (46)66 (47)55 (48)44 (49)66
(50)77 (51)77 (52)77 (53)88 (54)44 (55)44
(56)11 (57)11 (58)0 (59)66 (60)66
Page 71, Item 1:
(1)0 (2)99 (3)77 (4)77 (5)22 (6)22 (7)11
(8)0 (9)55 (10)66 (11)99 (12)88 (13)11
(14)55 (15)33 (16)66 (17)77 (18)55 (19)99
(20)33 (21)22 (22)99 (23)44 (24)33 (25)55
(26)33 (27)88 (28)66 (29)55 (30)44 (31)33
(32)88 (33)66 (34)55 (35)0 (36)88 (37)44
(38)0 (39)33 (40)33 (41)22 (42)11 (43)33
(44)22 (45)0 (46)11 (47)11 (48)22 (49)11
(50)44 (51)55 (52)22 (53)99 (54)55 (55)88
(56)11 (57)0 (58)0 (59)99 (60)77
Page 72, Item 1:
(1)33 (2)77 (3)55 (4)66 (5)55 (6)11 (7)55
(8)22 (9)0 (10)55 (11)88 (12)77 (13)44
(14)66 (15)22 (16)33 (17)88 (18)0 (19)33
(20)77 (21)44 (22)33 (23)44 (24)11 (25)33
(26)66 (27)22 (28)44 (29)55 (30)99 (31)11
(32)66 (33)77 (34)44 (35)55 (36)55 (37)44

(38)11 (39)77 (40)11 (41)11 (42)66 (43)33
(44)99 (45)11 (46)99 (47)66 (48)88 (49)22
(50)0 (51)66 (52)0 (53)22 (54)44 (55)55
(56)33 (57)55 (58)0 (59)33 (60)66
Page 73, Item 1:
(1)33 (2)33 (3)44 (4)44 (5)66 (6)44 (7)77
(8)0 (9)55 (10)55 (11)44 (12)33 (13)11
(14)44 (15)77 (16)55 (17)88 (18)11 (19)11
(20)11 (21)44 (22)88 (23)44 (24)11 (25)66
(26)88 (27)55 (28)11 (29)44 (30)22 (31)77
(32)11 (33)44 (34)77 (35)99 (36)77 (37)0
(38)22 (39)99 (40)77 (41)88 (42)77 (43)22
(44)0 (45)0 (46)33 (47)33 (48)0 (49)22
(50)55 (51)55 (52)33 (53)66 (54)0 (55)88
(56)22 (57)55 (58)99 (59)99 (60)0
Page 74, Item 1:
(1)22 (2)77 (3)66 (4)0 (5)77 (6)99 (7)55
(8)66 (9)77 (10)11 (11)66 (12)77 (13)44
(14)11 (15)33 (16)99 (17)99 (18)44 (19)44
(20)77 (21)55 (22)99 (23)22 (24)44 (25)33
(26)33 (27)88 (28)55 (29)88 (30)88 (31)77
(32)0 (33)44 (34)22 (35)0 (36)11 (37)22
(38)22 (39)22 (40)99 (41)99 (42)55 (43)66
(44)88 (45)11 (46)88 (47)44 (48)88 (49)77
(50)88 (51)33 (52)22 (53)55 (54)88 (55)55
(56)66 (57)55 (58)55 (59)44 (60)44
Page 75, Item 1:
(1)55 (2)88 (3)88 (4)33 (5)22 (6)55 (7)0
(8)55 (9)22 (10)11 (11)11 (12)55 (13)66

(14)55 (15)66 (16)77 (17)55 (18)22 (19)99
(20)44 (21)44 (22)77 (23)66 (24)33 (25)0
(26)44 (27)66 (28)11 (29)99 (30)44 (31)44
(32)22 (33)99 (34)55 (35)55 (36)22 (37)55
(38)88 (39)99 (40)44 (41)55 (42)55 (43)44
(44)0 (45)44 (46)11 (47)99 (48)88 (49)99
(50)88 (51)33 (52)22 (53)77 (54)88 (55)55
(56)22 (57)22 (58)22 (59)88 (60)99

Page 76, Item 1:

(1)24 (2)84 (3)96 (4)84 (5)12 (6)72 (7)108
(8)0 (9)84 (10)84 (11)24 (12)60 (13)24
(14)108 (15)12 (16)72 (17)36 (18)24 (19)12
(20)108 (21)24 (22)48 (23)0 (24)108 (25)60
(26)96 (27)12 (28)0 (29)36 (30)108 (31)24
(32)96 (33)12 (34)48 (35)12 (36)84 (37)24
(38)24 (39)96 (40)12 (41)72 (42)108 (43)36
(44)48 (45)108 (46)24 (47)12 (48)72 (49)0
(50)72 (51)36 (52)84 (53)72 (54)48 (55)12
(56)12 (57)96 (58)12 (59)12 (60)96

Page 77, Item 1:

(1)108 (2)12 (3)96 (4)60 (5)60 (6)96 (7)60
(8)48 (9)48 (10)72 (11)108 (12)36 (13)24
(14)60 (15)96 (16)48 (17)36 (18)12 (19)0
(20)60 (21)96 (22)60 (23)84 (24)72 (25)60
(26)24 (27)108 (28)60 (29)36 (30)96
(31)108 (32)48 (33)24 (34)60 (35)36 (36)0
(37)72 (38)84 (39)48 (40)96 (41)108 (42)0
(43)48 (44)96 (45)72 (46)72 (47)84 (48)0
(49)0 (50)84 (51)96 (52)108 (53)36 (54)48
(55)108 (56)108 (57)72 (58)96 (59)108
(60)36

Page 78, Item 1:

(1)108 (2)36 (3)60 (4)24 (5)60 (6)84 (7)36
(8)72 (9)24 (10)48 (11)60 (12)84 (13)36
(14)24 (15)0 (16)84 (17)36 (18)36 (19)48
(20)48 (21)96 (22)96 (23)24 (24)84 (25)96
(26)96 (27)24 (28)84 (29)84 (30)0 (31)84
(32)12 (33)96 (34)24 (35)36 (36)96 (37)24
(38)60 (39)0 (40)48 (41)0 (42)108 (43)36
(44)0 (45)96 (46)84 (47)96 (48)24 (49)84
(50)24 (51)24 (52)60 (53)96 (54)60 (55)60
(56)96 (57)24 (58)48 (59)0 (60)12

Page 79, Item 1:

(1)84 (2)24 (3)60 (4)84 (5)72 (6)24 (7)0
(8)84 (9)12 (10)84 (11)108 (12)0 (13)48
(14)108 (15)24 (16)48 (17)36 (18)36 (19)48
(20)0 (21)36 (22)48 (23)12 (24)0 (25)48
(26)72 (27)0 (28)0 (29)12 (30)108 (31)72

(32)60 (33)12 (34)36 (35)108 (36)84 (37)12
(38)24 (39)72 (40)96 (41)60 (42)48 (43)84
(44)84 (45)48 (46)96 (47)36 (48)12 (49)48
(50)24 (51)108 (52)60 (53)108 (54)48
(55)48 (56)84 (57)12 (58)12 (59)72 (60)0

Page 80, Item 1:

(1)48 (2)0 (3)96 (4)96 (5)48 (6)48 (7)36
(8)72 (9)24 (10)96 (11)36 (12)36 (13)96
(14)72 (15)96 (16)36 (17)108 (18)48 (19)84
(20)12 (21)36 (22)72 (23)12 (24)72 (25)12
(26)60 (27)36 (28)48 (29)36 (30)60 (31)48
(32)108 (33)96 (34)84 (35)36 (36)48 (37)60
(38)0 (39)96 (40)12 (41)108 (42)96 (43)36
(44)36 (45)84 (46)84 (47)24 (48)84 (49)72
(50)84 (51)36 (52)108 (53)36 (54)108 (55)0
(56)96 (57)12 (58)24 (59)84 (60)60

Page 81, Item 1:

(1)24 (2)96 (3)96 (4)72 (5)24 (6)96 (7)108
(8)60 (9)0 (10)24 (11)84 (12)108 (13)12
(14)0 (15)12 (16)48 (17)108 (18)12 (19)12
(20)84 (21)24 (22)0 (23)72 (24)0 (25)60
(26)0 (27)0 (28)84 (29)108 (30)36 (31)0
(32)36 (33)72 (34)108 (35)108 (36)96
(37)24 (38)96 (39)36 (40)96 (41)24 (42)96
(43)24 (44)24 (45)36 (46)72 (47)60 (48)84
(49)0 (50)72 (51)84 (52)72 (53)72 (54)0
(55)60 (56)24 (57)0 (58)72 (59)108 (60)48

Page 82, Item 1:

(1)24 (2)72 (3)84 (4)48 (5)48 (6)84 (7)72
(8)36 (9)108 (10)72 (11)60 (12)84 (13)12

(14)0 (15)96 (16)36 (17)72 (18)108 (19)72
(20)72 (21)84 (22)108 (23)0 (24)0 (25)108
(26)84 (27)96 (28)84 (29)0 (30)24 (31)108
(32)96 (33)12 (34)96 (35)108 (36)84 (37)48
(38)48 (39)108 (40)36 (41)36 (42)72 (43)0
(44)12 (45)12 (46)72 (47)36 (48)84 (49)60
(50)48 (51)60 (52)24 (53)24 (54)84 (55)36
(56)24 (57)24 (58)72 (59)24 (60)72

Page 83, Item 1:

(1)84 (2)40 (3)24 (4)16 (5)3 (6)15 (7)18
(8)63 (9)72 (10)0 (11)54 (12)1 (13)0 (14)7
(15)0 (16)96 (17)6 (18)0 (19)21 (20)56
(21)12 (22)25 (23)0 (24)110 (25)0 (26)6
(27)100 (28)10 (29)20 (30)12 (31)0 (32)8
(33)0 (34)6 (35)42 (36)18 (37)8 (38)110
(39)15 (40)9 (41)14 (42)42 (43)12 (44)10
(45)84 (46)36 (47)0 (48)0 (49)36 (50)8
(51)63 (52)81 (53)35 (54)96 (55)44 (56)55
(57)63 (58)15 (59)0 (60)120

Page 84, Item 1:

(1)15 (2)44 (3)72 (4)0 (5)0 (6)36 (7)2 (8)8
(9)0 (10)96 (11)9 (12)6 (13)28 (14)48
(15)32 (16)40 (17)0 (18)0 (19)80 (20)80
(21)25 (22)24 (23)24 (24)0 (25)63 (26)16
(27)4 (28)40 (29)12 (30)30 (31)0 (32)90
(33)24 (34)0 (35)10 (36)36 (37)2 (38)12
(39)0 (40)8 (41)6 (42)6 (43)50 (44)108
(45)100 (46)60 (47)9 (48)0 (49)90 (50)3
(51)0 (52)20 (53)42 (54)54 (55)8 (56)12
(57)4 (58)45 (59)0 (60)49

Page 85, Item 1:

(1)40 (2)20 (3)64 (4)12 (5)8 (6)4 (7)15
(8)20 (9)42 (10)50 (11)27 (12)28 (13)0
(14)60 (15)4 (16)0 (17)99 (18)99 (19)21
(20)12 (21)54 (22)60 (23)16 (24)18 (25)0
(26)20 (27)8 (28)60 (29)8 (30)48 (31)80
(32)42 (33)3 (34)60 (35)15 (36)40 (37)99
(38)22 (39)16 (40)10 (41)4 (42)11 (43)48
(44)4 (45)48 (46)12 (47)96 (48)0 (49)9
(50)0 (51)27 (52)15 (53)14 (54)49 (55)0
(56)88 (57)0 (58)10 (59)0 (60)24

Page 86, Item 1:

(1)0 (2)0 (3)48 (4)0 (5)10 (6)2 (7)14 (8)0
(9)45 (10)8 (11)60 (12)56 (13)50 (14)12
(15)24 (16)36 (17)56 (18)50 (19)110 (20)0
(21)12 (22)0 (23)49 (24)14 (25)5 (26)0
(27)110 (28)80 (29)50 (30)2 (31)25 (32)72
(33)0 (34)45 (35)25 (36)36 (37)5 (38)30

(39)27 (40)88 (41)81 (42)32 (43)40 (44)36
(45)10 (46)12 (47)15 (48)50 (49)88 (50)72
(51)60 (52)12 (53)35 (54)66 (55)7 (56)12
(57)0 (58)10 (59)70 (60)6

Page 87, Item 1:

(1)50 (2)30 (3)0 (4)9 (5)0 (6)77 (7)54
(8)120 (9)5 (10)70 (11)12 (12)11 (13)30
(14)108 (15)54 (16)15 (17)18 (18)54 (19)10
(20)63 (21)15 (22)0 (23)30 (24)36 (25)2
(26)80 (27)5 (28)24 (29)12 (30)36 (31)12
(32)45 (33)12 (34)45 (35)66 (36)12 (37)12
(38)66 (39)12 (40)0 (41)0 (42)0 (43)48
(44)8 (45)44 (46)6 (47)42 (48)0 (49)110
(50)15 (51)0 (52)0 (53)9 (54)0 (55)0 (56)18
(57)7 (58)88 (59)110 (60)15

Page 88, Item 1:

(1)30 (2)24 (3)96 (4)0 (5)24 (6)64 (7)5
(8)33 (9)0 (10)110 (11)96 (12)40 (13)84
(14)8 (15)21 (16)16 (17)0 (18)54 (19)120
(20)24 (21)63 (22)77 (23)60 (24)33 (25)0
(26)70 (27)0 (28)12 (29)50 (30)9 (31)0
(32)99 (33)6 (34)60 (35)0 (36)18 (37)5
(38)5 (39)6 (40)0 (41)48 (42)30 (43)6
(44)42 (45)20 (46)0 (47)0 (48)0 (49)6
(50)28 (51)0 (52)28 (53)10 (54)35 (55)84
(56)0 (57)50 (58)0 (59)40 (60)0

Page 89, Item 1:

(1)5 (2)0 (3)15 (4)3 (5)44 (6)25 (7)70 (8)50
(9)10 (10)20 (11)54 (12)99 (13)0 (14)44

(15)25 (16)9 (17)80 (18)84 (19)6 (20)4
(21)14 (22)0 (23)72 (24)18 (25)90 (26)120
(27)56 (28)12 (29)18 (30)11 (31)60 (32)0
(33)18 (34)0 (35)72 (36)6 (37)36 (38)0
(39)100 (40)4 (41)70 (42)22 (43)18 (44)84
(45)8 (46)16 (47)12 (48)0 (49)50 (50)64
(51)120 (52)25 (53)90 (54)54 (55)84 (56)63
(57)0 (58)18 (59)0 (60)60

Page 90, Item 1:
(1)72 (2)30 (3)56 (4)60 (5)7 (6)42 (7)44
(8)72 (9)90 (10)28 (11)21 (12)16 (13)110
(14)88 (15)9 (16)24 (17)30 (18)22 (19)0
(20)0 (21)22 (22)66 (23)4 (24)48 (25)3
(26)12 (27)0 (28)48 (29)20 (30)0 (31)0
(32)36 (33)108 (34)16 (35)28 (36)56 (37)18
(38)16 (39)100 (40)5 (41)60 (42)18 (43)24
(44)9 (45)6 (46)4 (47)0 (48)0 (49)36 (50)0
(51)45 (52)21 (53)100 (54)10 (55)63 (56)2
(57)0 (58)55 (59)16 (60)0

Page 91, Item 1:
(1)36 (2)44 (3)50 (4)40 (5)60 (6)120 (7)44
(8)0 (9)18 (10)0 (11)80 (12)16 (13)16 (14)7
(15)36 (16)48 (17)60 (18)35 (19)55 (20)0
(21)25 (22)90 (23)54 (24)21 (25)35 (26)35
(27)35 (28)40 (29)108 (30)90 (31)24 (32)90
(33)60 (34)36 (35)100 (36)0 (37)0 (38)5
(39)77 (40)8 (41)88 (42)2 (43)56 (44)88
(45)72 (46)4 (47)28 (48)16 (49)32 (50)48
(51)6 (52)0 (53)5 (54)55 (55)33 (56)9 (57)9
(58)10 (59)10 (60)9

Page 92, Item 1:
(1)3 (2)30 (3)0 (4)16 (5)0 (6)4 (7)110 (8)30
(9)36 (10)120 (11)4 (12)120 (13)20 (14)0
(15)40 (16)12 (17)84 (18)48 (19)0 (20)110
(21)32 (22)120 (23)12 (24)40 (25)30 (26)33
(27)49 (28)12 (29)36 (30)56 (31)0 (32)0
(33)60 (34)36 (35)16 (36)0 (37)12 (38)24
(39)64 (40)0 (41)20 (42)66 (43)8 (44)0
(45)3 (46)16 (47)36 (48)12 (49)30 (50)28
(51)70 (52)32 (53)70 (54)64 (55)45 (56)42

(57)8 (58)3 (59)14 (60)90

Page 93, Item 1:
(1)18 (2)81 (3)25 (4)30 (5)0 (6)33 (7)6 (8)0
(9)0 (10)16 (11)0 (12)36 (13)0 (14)72
(15)56 (16)11 (17)10 (18)36 (19)0 (20)12
(21)36 (22)0 (23)42 (24)8 (25)30 (26)54
(27)30 (28)6 (29)90 (30)66 (31)6 (32)0
(33)110 (34)28 (35)35 (36)12 (37)0 (38)63
(39)63 (40)8 (41)90 (42)8 (43)50 (44)42
(45)0 (46)15 (47)80 (48)48 (49)24 (50)80
(51)15 (52)0 (53)18 (54)36 (55)88 (56)10
(57)0 (58)24 (59)20 (60)24

Page 94, Item 1:
(1)99 (2)48 (3)0 (4)0 (5)0 (6)15 (7)4 (8)0
(9)18 (10)0 (11)72 (12)10 (13)7 (14)21
(15)24 (16)24 (17)15 (18)56 (19)0 (20)5
(21)36 (22)10 (23)45 (24)2 (25)88 (26)0
(27)0 (28)0 (29)0 (30)4 (31)100 (32)4 (33)0
(34)81 (35)12 (36)30 (37)4 (38)63 (39)90
(40)4 (41)2 (42)32 (43)100 (44)54 (45)4
(46)0 (47)0 (48)0 (49)24 (50)6 (51)24
(52)120 (53)5 (54)8 (55)0 (56)99 (57)0
(58)8 (59)48 (60)48

Page 95, Item 1:
(1)66 (2)12 (3)0 (4)0 (5)50 (6)49 (7)16 (8)0
(9)63 (10)12 (11)15 (12)6 (13)0 (14)21
(15)40 (16)56 (17)63 (18)21 (19)0 (20)36
(21)27 (22)30 (23)12 (24)0 (25)80 (26)24
(27)0 (28)64 (29)64 (30)48 (31)120 (32)108

(33)12 (34)12 (35)120 (36)9 (37)5 (38)28
(39)20 (40)10 (41)35 (42)30 (43)0 (44)35
(45)0 (46)32 (47)4 (48)42 (49)36 (50)80
(51)28 (52)36 (53)10 (54)0 (55)0 (56)4
(57)60 (58)6 (59)90 (60)66

Page 96, Item 1:

(1)18 (2)60 (3)22 (4)88 (5)20 (6)0 (7)100
(8)22 (9)24 (10)64 (11)80 (12)18 (13)0
(14)12 (15)0 (16)20 (17)0 (18)18 (19)0
(20)1 (21)54 (22)27 (23)0 (24)0 (25)30
(26)0 (27)60 (28)36 (29)12 (30)54 (31)0
(32)24 (33)90 (34)70 (35)84 (36)81 (37)0
(38)36 (39)5 (40)45 (41)10 (42)32 (43)8
(44)36 (45)8 (46)50 (47)4 (48)28 (49)20
(50)9 (51)0 (52)18 (53)36 (54)0 (55)60
(56)30 (57)30 (58)8 (59)12 (60)4

Page 97, Item 1:

(1)56 (2)40 (3)3 (4)96 (5)27 (6)18 (7)24
(8)90 (9)0 (10)48 (11)30 (12)15 (13)0 (14)0
(15)9 (16)8 (17)70 (18)16 (19)3 (20)16
(21)50 (22)10 (23)50 (24)88 (25)120 (26)36
(27)60 (28)5 (29)9 (30)77 (31)40 (32)40
(33)40 (34)20 (35)30 (36)10 (37)0 (38)0
(39)21 (40)6 (41)9 (42)56 (43)0 (44)8
(45)50 (46)0 (47)32 (48)60 (49)8 (50)2
(51)30 (52)24 (53)0 (54)50 (55)9 (56)63
(57)16 (58)28 (59)36 (60)36

Page 98, Item 1:

(1)40 (2)7 (3)35 (4)36 (5)10 (6)50 (7)33
(8)5 (9)16 (10)0 (11)0 (12)32 (13)45 (14)0
(15)66 (16)110 (17)5 (18)24 (19)100 (20)99
(21)6 (22)12 (23)6 (24)54 (25)0 (26)0
(27)27 (28)30 (29)72 (30)72 (31)36 (32)45
(33)110 (34)0 (35)8 (36)60 (37)120 (38)63
(39)24 (40)20 (41)0 (42)77 (43)36 (44)90
(45)28 (46)77 (47)5 (48)28 (49)6 (50)48
(51)60 (52)64 (53)60 (54)88 (55)2 (56)27
(57)56 (58)0 (59)0 (60)56

Page 99, Item 1:

(1)54 (2)42 (3)0 (4)24 (5)0 (6)10 (7)49

(8)32 (9)16 (10)6 (11)24 (12)11 (13)18
(14)0 (15)72 (16)60 (17)110 (18)0 (19)21
(20)0 (21)36 (22)45 (23)44 (24)0 (25)80
(26)0 (27)42 (28)6 (29)0 (30)12 (31)99
(32)0 (33)6 (34)40 (35)77 (36)0 (37)16
(38)110 (39)42 (40)4 (41)10 (42)21 (43)35
(44)72 (45)0 (46)64 (47)0 (48)45 (49)1
(50)16 (51)0 (52)0 (53)3 (54)6 (55)20
(56)10 (57)4 (58)18 (59)8 (60)20

Page 100, Item 1:

(1)42 (2)110 (3)8 (4)99 (5)110 (6)0 (7)80
(8)16 (9)0 (10)0 (11)4 (12)100 (13)6 (14)24
(15)7 (16)25 (17)18 (18)36 (19)0 (20)99
(21)12 (22)12 (23)12 (24)6 (25)6 (26)0
(27)9 (28)99 (29)6 (30)50 (31)54 (32)16
(33)15 (34)16 (35)32 (36)9 (37)18 (38)10
(39)40 (40)120 (41)45 (42)45 (43)42 (44)12
(45)64 (46)28 (47)90 (48)40 (49)18 (50)7
(51)80 (52)12 (53)45 (54)72 (55)25 (56)20
(57)16 (58)12 (59)0 (60)55

LEAVE A REVIEW

THANK YOU SO MUCH FOR PURCHASING OUR BOOK.

IF YOU LIKE THIS MATH WORKBOOK, THEN DO LEAVE YOUR VALUABLE REVIEW ON AMAZON ABOUT THIS BOOK.

WE ARE A HOME BASED PUBLISHING COMPNAY AND DON'T A HUGE ADVERTISING BUDGET, YOUR REVIEW CAN REALLY HELP US SHOW THIS BOOK TO OTHERS.

THANK YOU AGAIN!

ESHAAL MATHS

CHECKOUT MORE MATH BOOKS BY ESHAAL MATHS

JUST SCAN THE QR CODE ABOVE!

THANKS!

Made in the USA
Coppell, TX
31 May 2024

32949118R00072